P9-DCR-990

NATIONAL AUDUBON SOCIETY®

FIRST
FIELD
GUIDE
AMPHIBIANS

NATIONAL AUDUBON SOCIETY®

FIRST
FIELD
GUIDE
AMPHIBIANS

Written by
Brian Cassie

Scholastic Inc.

New York Toronto London Auckland Sydney
Mexico City New Delhi Hong Kong

The National Audubon Society, established in
1905, has 550,000 members and more than 500
chapters nationwide. Its mission is to conserve
and restore natural ecosystems, focusing on
wildlife and plant life, and these guides are part
of that mission. Celebrating the beauty and wonders of nature,
Audubon looks toward its second century of educating people of
all ages. For information about Audubon membership, contact:

National Audubon Society
700 Broadway
New York, NY 10003-9562
800-274-4201
http://www.audubon.org/

Copyright © 1999 by Chanticleer Press, Inc.
All rights reserved. Published by Scholastic Inc.
SCHOLASTIC and associated logos are trademarks and/or registered trademarks of
Scholastic Inc.

LIBRARY OF CONGRESS CATALOGING-IN-PUBLICATION DATA

Cassie, Brian, 1953–
    National Audubon Society first field guide. Amphibians / by Brian Cassie.
        p.   cm.
    Includes bibliographical references (p.   ) and index.
    Summary: Explores the world of amphibians, discussing their classification,
anatomy, behavior, and habitat, and providing photographs and detailed
descriptions of individual species.
    ISBN 0-590-63982-X (hc). — ISBN 0-590-64008-9 (pb)
    1. Amphibians—Juvenile literature. 2. Amphibians—United States—
Identification—Juvenile literature. 3. Amphibians—
Canada—Identification—Juvenile literature. [1. Amphibians.]
I. Title.
QL644.2.C37 1999
597.8'0973—dc21   98-40931   CIP   AC

10 9 8 7 6 5 4 3 2   0/0   01   02   03

Printed in Hong Kong 54
First printing, August 1999
Front cover photograph: Pine Barrens Treefrog (Hyla andersonii) by C. Allan Morgan
National Audubon Society® is a registered trademark of National Audubon Society,
Inc., all rights reserved.

Contents

About this book

Spotted Salamander (page 108) with eggs

Whether you are watching frogs in your own backyard, or looking for salamanders in the woods, this book will help you learn to look at amphibians the way a naturalist does. This book is divided into four parts:

PART 1: The world of amphibians gives you lots of interesting information about amphibians, such as how they are named and what makes them perfectly suited to a variety of water and land habitats.

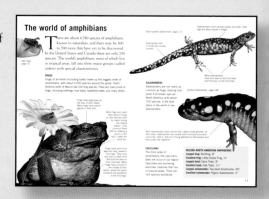

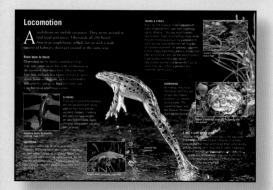

PART 2: How to look at amphibians tells you what you need to know to begin identifying amphibians—including what they look like, how they eat, move, and produce young, and where they live.

PART 3: The field guide includes detailed descriptions, range maps, and dramatic photographs of 50 common North American amphibians. In addition, this section provides helpful shorter descriptions accompanied by photographs of more than 85 other important species and subspecies.

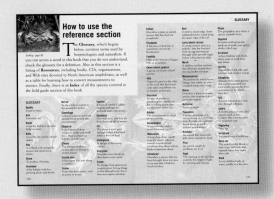

PART 4: The reference section at the back of the book includes a helpful glossary of terms used by naturalists when they talk about amphibians; lists of useful books, CDs, Web sites, and organizations; and an index of species covered in the field guide.

What is a naturalist?

A naturalist is a person who is very interested in nature and shares her or his enthusiasm and knowledge with others. People who study amphibians and reptiles professionally are known as herpetologists. The word *herpetologist* comes from the Greek word for creeping or crawling. Many herpetologists call reptiles and amphibians "herps."

NATURALISTS AND TEACHERS
David and Marvalee Wake are biologists (scientists who study living things) and professors at the University of California at Berkeley. In sharing their knowledge about the natural world, the Wakes have taught and guided many field researchers from the United States and around the globe. Amphibians and their survival are an important area of interest for the Wakes.

YOU CAN BE A NATURALIST, TOO.
Most naturalists enjoy nature as a hobby and not as a full-time job. You can be a naturalist yourself.

Essential equipment

Amphibian watchers need a few essential tools in the field. A field guide, such as this one, will help you identify the creatures you find. A notebook and pencils are important, too. Writing notes is a key to being a good naturalist. Sketching pictures, or taking photographs, is also useful and fun. Binoculars can be very helpful for tracking frogs at ponds, a flashlight or headlamp is essential for spotting amphibians at night, and a tape recorder can be used for recording and playing frog calls. Rubber boots or old sneakers are good choices for footwear when exploring for amphibians.

Rules for amphibian watchers

- When you go out exploring, take a buddy along and tell a grown-up where you are going. Go on nighttime searches with an adult.
- Always put back boards, stones, and other objects that you might move while searching for amphibians.
- Never remove amphibians from their homes; enjoy them where you find them.
- Always wash your hands after you have touched any amphibians; toxins in their skin can be painful if you rub your eyes.
- Never handle any amphibian if you have insect repellent or creams on your hands; they can have harmful effects on the animal.
- Make notes and share your discoveries with others. That makes them doubly exciting.

Long-toed Salamander larva page 107

What are amphibians?

Like birds, reptiles, mammals, and fishes, amphibians are vertebrates—that is, creatures with a backbone and an internal skeleton. While no one would ever mistake a frog for a bird, or a salamander for a squirrel, you might confuse a tadpole with a fish or a salamander with a lizard. What is it that separates amphibians from other vertebrates?

Amphibian features

Amphibians have no hair, scales, feathers, or claws—features that you find on other vertebrates. All amphibians have glands in their skin that produce mucus and other secretions to help keep their skin surface moist.

The Mudpuppy (page 98) has gills its whole life.

At some point in their lives, amphibians have gills, like fish, to help them breathe underwater. Usually, they have gills during the young phase of their existence, though adults retain gills in a few species.

Two lives

The term *amphibian* means two lives
and refers to the many amphibians
that start off life in water or in a
fluid-filled egg sac, breathing through
gills, and later leave the water to
become land-inhabiting adults. Some
amphibians do not live "two lives,"

Adult Green Frog page 97

*Young Green Treefrog
page 80*

however, but spend their whole lives either on land
or in water. But even the landlubbers must continue
to live near water, or at least in humid or moist
surroundings. All North American amphibians hatch
from eggs, undergo a larval period, change into
juveniles, and mature into adults. However, there is a
tremendous amount of variation in how different
amphibian species lead their lives.

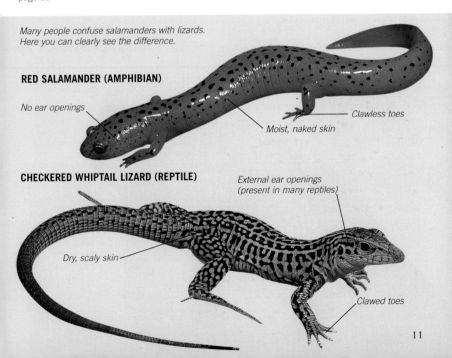

*Many people confuse salamanders with lizards.
Here you can clearly see the difference.*

RED SALAMANDER (AMPHIBIAN)

No ear openings

Clawless toes

Moist, naked skin

CHECKERED WHIPTAIL LIZARD (REPTILE)

External ear openings
(present in many reptiles)

Dry, scaly skin

Clawed toes

11

The world of amphibians

Oak Toad
page 70

There are about 4,780 species of amphibians known to naturalists, and there may be 300 to 500 more that have yet to be discovered. In the United States and Canada there are only 250 species. The world's amphibians, most of which live in tropical areas, fall into three major groups (called orders) with special characteristics.

FROGS

Frogs of all kinds (including toads) make up the biggest order of amphibians, with about 4,000 species around the globe. North America north of Mexico has 100 frog species. There are many kinds of frogs, including treefrogs, true toads, spadefoot toads, and many others.

Little Grass Frog page 87

Frogs have large eyes on the tops of their heads. Many frogs have poison glands in their skin.

Most frogs and toads have distinct songs or calls that are used by males during the mating season. They produce these calls by inflating a pouch in the neck, called the vocal sac.

Frogs have short front legs and long, powerful hind legs. They have four toes on their front feet and five toes on their hind feet. Many frogs have a hump in the middle of their backs, where the pelvis connects the backbone to the hind legs.

Cane Toad, page 72

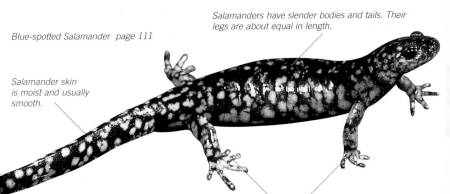

Blue-spotted Salamander page 111

Salamanders have slender bodies and tails. Their legs are about equal in length.

Salamander skin is moist and usually smooth.

Most salamanders have four toes on the front feet and five toes on the hind feet.

SALAMANDERS

Salamanders are not nearly as common as frogs, totaling only some 410 known species. North America, with about 150 species, is the best place in the world to see salamanders.

Spotted Salamander page 108

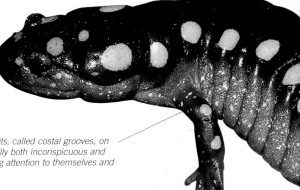

Most salamanders have vertical slits, called costal grooves, on their sides. Salamanders are usually both inconspicuous and nocturnal—that is, they don't bring attention to themselves and they prefer the nighttime.

CAECILIANS

The third order of amphibians, the caecilians, does not occur in our region. Caecilians are burrowing wormlike creatures that live in tropical areas. There are 165 species worldwide.

RECORD NORTH AMERICAN AMPHIBIANS
Largest frog: Bullfrog, 8"
Smallest frog: Little Grass Frog, ⅝"
Largest toad: Cane Toad, 9"
Smallest toad: Oak Toad, 1¼"
Largest salamander: Two-toed Amphiuma, 45"
Smallest salamander: Pygmy Salamander, 2"

What's in a name?

Living things, such as birds, insects, wildflowers, and amphibians, are classified by scientists into groups that have features in common. The first level of these groups is the kingdom. Every living thing is placed in either the plant kingdom, the animal kingdom, or one of a few other kingdoms devoted mainly to microscopic life-forms.

WHERE ANIMALS ARE KINGS

In the animal kingdom, there are millions of kinds of animals. To help sort out the different groups, scientists have worked out a series of group levels. At each level, the animals have features in common with one another. The levels are called phylum, class, order, family, genus, and species.

*Barking Treefrog
page 82*

Scientific and common names

Living creatures have a variety of names. When a scientist discovers a new species of animal, she or he gives it a scientific name. Scientific names have two parts, the genus and the species, in that order. Some creatures, such as the famous dinosaur *Tyrannosaurus rex*, are known only by their scientific names. Most familiar animals, though, are better known

Cave Salamander page 119

by their common names. For instance, *Felis catus* is known as the house cat and *Rana catesbeiana* as the Bullfrog. Some people prefer to use just scientific names, while others favor common names. This guide provides both common and scientific names.

TWO AMPHIBIANS CLASSIFIED

The Green Treefrog and the Eastern Tiger Salamander share the same kingdom, phylum, and class, but below that they are separated into different orders, families, genera (the plural of genus), and species.

KINGDOM	Animalia	**KINGDOM**	Animalia
PHYLUM	Chordata	**PHYLUM**	Chordata
CLASS	Amphibia	**CLASS**	Amphibia
ORDER	Anura	**ORDER**	Caudata
FAMILY	Hylidae	**FAMILY**	Ambystomatidae
GENUS	*Hyla*	**GENUS**	*Ambystoma*
SPECIES	*cinerea*	**SPECIES**	*tigrinum*
(Green Treefrog)		(Eastern Tiger Salamander)	

Eastern Narrowmouth Toad
page 50

NARROWMOUTH TOADS

have short legs; broad waists; small, pointed heads; smooth skin; and a fold of skin at the back of their heads.

Amphibian families

Each family of amphibians has characteristics that help us to separate it from other amphibian families. Look over the pictures of some typical frogs and toads (here) and salamanders (turn the page) and try to become familiar with the family field marks.

TRUE FROGS

have long legs, webbed hind feet, pointed toes, and, quite often, ridges along the sides of their backs. Their eardrums can be very large.

SPADEFOOT TOADS

are rather plump, like true toads, but lack the large poison glands, and have smoothish skin, eyes with vertical, catlike pupils, and a "spade" on each hind foot.

Plains Spadefoot
page 60

Northern Leopard Frog page 93

Pacific Treefrog page 76

TREEFROGS

are mostly small, with long slender legs and long toes with big toe pads similar to suction cups. They often have bright colors on their hind legs and the sides of their bodies. Most treefrogs can change the color of their bodies to blend in with their surroundings.

FROGS VS TOADS

The frog order is divided into families. Some of these families are called frogs and some are called toads. When people think of the difference between frogs and toads, they are thinking about two of those families, true frogs (water-dwellers with long legs and slimy skin) and true toads (short and squat landlubbers with dry, warty skin). But each family, whether frog or toad, has its own special features.

Greenhouse Frog page 54

TROPICAL FROGS

are so varied that it is hard to name specific characteristics to look for. There are hundreds of species in the world but only a few in North America.

TRUE TOADS

have plump bodies, short legs, dry and warty skin, and rounded faces with large glands on the sides of their heads. The glands contain a poison that gets released in the mouth of any animal that tries to eat a toad. In some species the poison is strong enough to kill a cat or dog.

Arizona Toad page 65

SIRENS

are long, slender salamanders that look very much like eels. They have one pair of small legs just behind the gills, and no hind legs.

Greater Siren
page 102

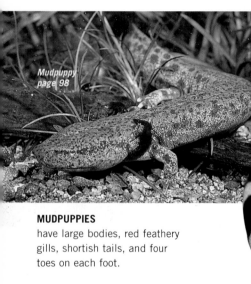

Mudpuppy
page 98

Marbled Salamander page 110

MUDPUPPIES

have large bodies, red feathery gills, shortish tails, and four toes on each foot.

AMPHIUMAS

look like eels with four very small legs. They have one to three toes per foot, depending on the species.

Three-toed Amphiuma
page 105

LUNGLESS SALAMANDERS,
the largest family, are varied but have the "typical" salamander shape—long, narrow body and short legs—a groove from the nostril to the upper lip, and noticeable costal grooves along the sides. They do not have lungs, but instead breathe through their skin.

Jordan's Salamander page 135

MOLE SALAMANDERS
are thick-bodied with wide heads, obvious costal grooves on their sides, no nostril-to-lip grooves, and rounded tails.

Hellbender page 100

HELLBENDERS
have massive bodies with folds of loose skin, large, flat heads, and short, thick legs.

NEWTS
have rougher skin than most other salamanders and no noticeable costal grooves. Eastern newts have colorful markings on their backs; western newts have brightly colored underparts. Young newts are called efts.

California Newt page 149

Amphibian senses

Animals relate to their surroundings through their sense organs. Like humans, amphibians have five senses— hearing, smell, sight, taste, and touch—and special organs that make these senses possible.

SIGHT

Amphibian eyes are usually well developed and obvious. A few species of salamanders are nearly blind, but most amphibians see very well. Land-dwelling species have eyelids; those that live in water have a thin membrane that covers the eyes. Eye color varies, as does the shape of the pupil. Some amphibians have narrow, slitlike pupils; others have large, round pupils. Most frogs have horizontal pupils.

Western Spadefoot's eye page 61

FROG EYES

All frogs have eyelids, and their eyes are big and bulgy. They can see in front, above, to the sides, and behind. This makes it difficult to sneak up on them. It also allows them to detect the slightest movement of an insect or other meal. But that's not all! Those huge eyes can be pulled down into the head—and through the roof of the mouth—where they help push big food items down the frog's throat.

Frogs can raise their eyes above water and keep their bodies hidden below.

TASTE

When it comes to taste, don't trust an amphibian. Although they have taste buds on their tongues and around the insides of their mouths, amphibians do not really care very much about the way something tastes—as long as it isn't poisonous.

SMELL

Amphibians smell with two sets of sense organs—one within the mouth, the other at the tip of the snout.

An American Toad (page 68) eating an earthworm

HEARING

Most species of frogs have well-developed ears and hear very well. The eardrum, called the tympanum, is located just behind the eye and is quite large and easy to see on a number of species. Salamanders have ears but "hear" mostly by detecting vibrations that pass through the ground or water.

The shed skin of an Eastern Tiger Salamander page 109

Male Bullfrog page 96

TOUCH

As with humans, the largest sense organ on an amphibian is its skin. Amphibian skin is supplied with small glands that secrete mucus to keep it moist and poison to keep the skin from tasting good to predators. Amphibians are so particular about their skin that they grow a new one as often as possible—at least every few days.

Amphibian behavior

You may never actually see a bunch of frogs playing a game of leapfrog, but amphibians do have a number of typical behavior patterns that are easy to observe if you have a little patience. Some can be seen any time the animals are active. Others can be appreciated only at a certain season or time of day.

BASKING IN THE SUN

Basking, or lounging in the sun, is the main way in which frogs keep their body temperatures at the right level. Amphibians are cold-blooded and depend on heat from their surroundings to warm them. This is why we see so few amphibians in cold weather—they cannot stay warm enough to be active.

Female Black Salamander (page 139) guarding her eggs

AMPHIBIAN PARENTS

Parenting is a behavior practiced by some salamanders and a few frogs. Actually, salamanders brood—or guard—their eggs until they hatch, but are not attentive to the young after that. Salamanders are much easier to find than their eggs, but if you find a batch of eggs, a mother will likely be near. Some salamanders, including the enormous Hellbender, can be very aggressive guarding their eggs.

FROGGIE GOES A'COURTIN'

Calling or singing is the most conspicuous amphibian behavior. It is practiced by almost all frogs, which call to let other frogs know where they are and when they are available for breeding.

22

AMPHIBIANS ON THE MARCH

Marching to pools created by spring rains and other temporary breeding sites is one of the most interesting amphibian behaviors to watch for. Depending on where you live and the time of year, you may observe mole salamanders, newts, true frogs, treefrogs, or spadefoot toads coming out of a period of inactivity and heading to their breeding pools during rainstorms.

Female California Newt (page 149) migrating toward breeding site

Spring Peeper (page 84) with expanded vocal sac

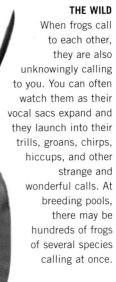

CALL OF THE WILD

When frogs call to each other, they are also unknowingly calling to you. You can often watch them as their vocal sacs expand and they launch into their trills, groans, chirps, hiccups, and other strange and wonderful calls. At breeding pools, there may be hundreds of frogs of several species calling at once.

The life cycle

The cycles of an amphibian's life are complex and fascinating. There are many variations in the life cycles of different species, but all North American amphibians hatch from eggs, undergo a larval period, change into juveniles in a process called metamorphosis, and mature into adults.

The egg comes first

All amphibians begin life as an egg. Amphibians spend varying amounts of time in the egg (from hours to weeks), depending on the type of amphibian and the climate in which it lives.

6.
The fully developed Pacific Treefrog lives in vegetation near its watery breeding grounds.

Adult Pacific Treefrog page 76

5.
With its metamorphosis nearly complete, the Pacific Treefrog tadpole prepares for life as a land-dweller.

4.
As it grows, the tadpole begins to metamorphose (change) into a frog.

Life in the egg

Inside the walls of the egg, a frog or salamander begins to take shape and grow. Some amphibians that develop in eggs laid on land do not hatch until they are mature. They go through a larval (immature) stage right inside the egg. The egg provides them with the watery habitat they need.

Youth

Young frogs, known as tadpoles or pollywogs, leave their eggs when they are still larvae— or immature amphibians—and develop more fully in outside environments. Some larval salamanders also develop outside the egg.

Growing up

As young amphibians grow, they develop all their adult organs. Even after they appear to be adults—with fully developed legs and other organs—young amphibians have a lot of growing to do before they are mature enough to claim territories and mate.

1. The Pacific Treefrog life cycle begins when the female lays her eggs underwater (right).

2. After a few days, the Pacific Treefrog eggs show the developing larvae.

3. Within three to five weeks, the Pacific Treefrog eggs hatch into tadpoles.

25

Reproduction and egg laying

When amphibians become fully mature, they develop strong mating instincts. This is a good thing, because if they did not, all the species would become extinct. Reproduction is a critical process in the lives of all amphibians, and how they go about it is fascinating.

The male chorus

In the proper season, which is different depending upon the species, the temperature and humidity are just right for frogs to mate. Males gather at breeding sites—ponds, small rain pools, or just about any kind of standing water—and begin to call for female mates. This is called the male chorus, and as more and more males join in, it can grow to a very large size.

American Toads (page 68) and strands of eggs

Two male Great Plains Toads (page 63) challenging each other at breeding site

The salamander dance

Salamanders have their own way of making sure there are future generations. In order to get a female interested in him, a male salamander rubs himself against the female and puts on an elaborate performance.

FOLLOW ME!

If a female salamander likes a male's display, she will follow the male until he deposits a pyramid-shaped packet of sperm, called a spermatophore, on the ground. The female then places the spermatophore in an opening on the underside of her body called the cloaca. With fertilization ensured, she finds a place to lay her eggs.

SALAMANDER EGGS

Salamanders lay few eggs compared to frogs, but they tend to guard their eggs (frogs do not), and this helps them to hatch successfully. The eggs tend to be larger than frog eggs, offering more food for the developing salamander.

FROG EGGS

When a male and female frog finally choose each other as mates, they lock into an embrace called amplexus, with the male above the back of the female, his forelegs wrapped around her body. As the female releases her eggs into the water, the male covers them with his sperm, fertilizing them.

Wood Frog eggs (left) and Spotted Salamander eggs (right)

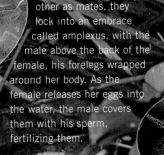

27

Daily life

Amphibians like rainy summer nights. But did you ever wonder how they get through the hot, dry days of summer and the freezing cold of winter?

Ensatina (page 142) hunting at night

Amphibians for all seasons

Depending on the environment in which they live, amphibians have various ways of making it through the year. Those salamanders and frogs that live in moist, warm, subtropical climates stay active throughout the year. The weather is always great for them. Farther north, in areas where winter temperatures fall below freezing and perhaps below zero, amphibians are active only during warm-weather months. During extended cold periods, they dig themselves into the ground and go through a phase similar to hibernation (called brumation in amphibians), during which they breathe just enough to stay alive and live off their body fat.

Desert amphibians

Desert-dwelling amphibians have to deal with winter cold and dry summer heat, both of which are deadly to most amphibians. They tend to spend a great deal of time in underground burrows, both in winter and summer, and emerge for extended periods only during times of heavy rain.

The daily grind

Most amphibians prefer twilight and nighttime for their periods of greatest activity. Nighttime is generally the most humid time of day, and the darkness serves as cover from predators. A number of frogs can be found basking in sunlight on riverbanks and lily pads, but the majority of North American amphibians do their hunting and courting when the lights are low.

Spring Peeper (page 84) in burrow

Squirrel Treefrog (page 81) calling in pond at night

LIFE SPANS
Scientists have found that in the wild, most small amphibians live about three to six years, most larger species up to eight years. Sirens and amphiumas may live to be 15 or so. Some mole salamanders are known to live up to 25 years.

Diet

All adult amphibians are meat eaters, or carnivores. They actively search for other animals—usually insects—to eat. Larval salamanders are also meat eaters. Most larval frogs are plant eaters, or vegetarians, although a few eat both plants and small animals.

Tailed Frog tadpole page 56

TADPOLE CARNIVORES
All tadpoles have special scraping mouthparts that are used for feeding on algae. Tadpoles of a few species, especially the spadefoot toads, sometimes become cannibals. They often eat their fellow tadpoles and can grow to enormous size, much larger than their vegetarian brothers and sisters.

Treefrog leaping at prey

Young Bullfrog (page 96) eating an earthworm

AS LONG AS IT'S WIGGLING...

Amphibians generally are not very particular about what they eat. Just about anything that is alive and fits in their mouth is fair game for adult salamanders and frogs. Some invertebrates (creatures without backbones), such as spiders, snails, worms, insects, and crayfish, are common in amphibian habitats and are eaten regularly. Narrowmouth toads are one of the few amphibians that eat mostly one thing. They specialize in eating ants.

Eastern Tiger Salamander (page 109) eating another salamander

CANNIBALS

Amphibians will eat many types of creatures. Fishes, reptiles, snails, baby birds—even other amphibians—are gobbled down if the opportunity arises.

A mphibians are mobile creatures. They move around to find food and mates. Obviously all 250 North American amphibians, which live in such a wide variety of habitats, don't get around in the same way.

From here to there

Depending on the family, amphibians hop, leap, run, jump, swim, flip, walk, and burrow in the course of their daily lives. They use their legs, feet, and tails in a variety of ways to move about. Some amphibians, such as salamanders and tadpoles, can grow back lost limbs and toes, but most adult frogs cannot.

Allegheny Dusky Salamander climbing page 117

CLIMBING

Climbing is not just for treefrogs, who are equipped with sticky pads on their toes and are excellent climbers; climbing and web-toed salamanders are also fine climbers. Some climbing salamanders use their tails as props.

SWIMMING

Swimming is one way larval salamanders, tadpoles, and some adult salamanders move about in their watery homes. In amphibian larvae and aquatic—or water-dwelling—salamanders, the tail has top and bottom fins, is flattened along the sides, and is the chief organ of propulsion in swimming.

Eastern Newt swimming (page 146)

TAKING A STROLL

Running, not hopping, helps narrowmouth toads disappear from sight with surprising speed. Walking is the way most lungless salamanders, toads, and treefrogs move when they are not being pursued by a predator. In land-dwelling salamanders the tail may also be used for movement. Its sideways, wavelike motions help propel these animals through leaf litter, among rocks, and over the ground surface. Flipping does not really get slender salamanders very far, but by rapidly flipping about they can confuse a predator and sometimes get to cover.

Jordan's Salamander (page 135) walking on forest floor

BURROWING

Burrowing, or burying themselves with the aid of specially shaped hind feet, is common among toads. The spadefoot toads and the Mexican Burrowing Toad are the best at it.

Couch's Spadefoot (page 59) burrowing into the ground

Leopard frog jumping

A HOP, A LEAP, AND A JUMP

Hopping with their short hind legs is the way many true toads move around when they are in a hurry. Long-legged true frogs and cricket frogs jump quickly and far, making them very hard to catch. Leaping is an act of desperation for true frogs, who leap into ponds and streams when they are frightened, and for treefrogs, who leap off their perches if they are in danger.

Defense

Compared to other vertebrates, which may be faster and stronger or possess poisonous bites or sharp claws, amphibians are relatively easy prey. In water and on land, they are pursued by a hungry throng of birds, mammals, reptiles, fishes, and other amphibians. Yet they have managed to survive for millions of years.

Amphibian armor

Amphibians don't have fangs and talons, but their subtle defense systems still function well. They have relatively small, slippery bodies and a generally quiet and retiring nature. Many species don't show themselves in daylight. Amphibians also have other survival tricks, many involving coloration.

Roughskin Newt (page 148) flashing its colors

FLASHING

Flash coloration is different from warning coloration because it is not seen until the amphibian is under attack. The bright colors distract and confuse predators and help the amphibians escape.

POISONS

Many amphibians produce mild skin poisons, and some secretions are toxic enough to kill predators. In salamanders, the tail is often the most poisonous part (and the part predators can most easily grab).

The Colorado River Toad (page 73) has poison glands behind the eyes.

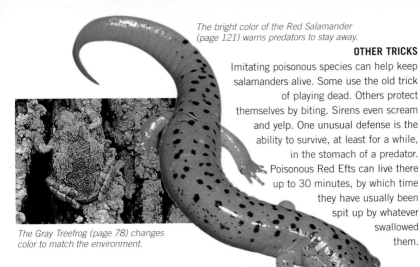
The bright color of the Red Salamander (page 121) warns predators to stay away.

OTHER TRICKS

Imitating poisonous species can help keep salamanders alive. Some use the old trick of playing dead. Others protect themselves by biting. Sirens even scream and yelp. One unusual defense is the ability to survive, at least for a while, in the stomach of a predator. Poisonous Red Efts can live there up to 30 minutes, by which time they have usually been spit up by whatever swallowed them.

The Gray Treefrog (page 78) changes color to match the environment.

COLOR-CHANGE ARTISTS

Changing skin coloration is employed by frogs, toads, and some salamanders. Treefrogs and other color-change artists change their colors over time to match the background they rest upon.

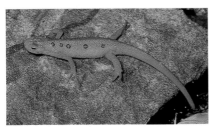

If eaten, the poisonous Red Eft (immature Eastern Newt; page 146) will make predators sick.

STANDING OUT

Warning coloration is the opposite of protective coloration. Bright colors on the upper surface of the skin usually mean the amphibian has quite poisonous skin. Predators who attack a brightly colored amphibian quickly learn to avoid similar-looking ones in the future.

Canyon Treefrog (page 77) blends into granite.

BLENDING IN

Protective coloration is important to many amphibians, a large number of which are green, brown, or gray—colors that are common in nature. These color patterns act as camouflage, helping amphibians blend in with their surroundings.

35

Northern Leopard Frog page 93

PONDS AND LAKES

Ponds and lakes, permanent
bodies of water, attract many
amphibians if there is lots of
vegetation in the shallows
and around the pond edges.
Eastern Newts, American
Toads, and many frogs,
including the Northern
Leopard and the Oregon
Spotted, can be found here.

California Giant Salamander
page 106

STREAMS

Streams are great habitats for
amphibians. Flat stones along
the edges of streams hide
Northern Two-lined and Spring
Salamanders in the East. In
the West, Tailed Frogs and
California Giant Salamanders
inhabit fast-flowing streams.
Mudpuppies and Hellbenders
live in deeper waters.

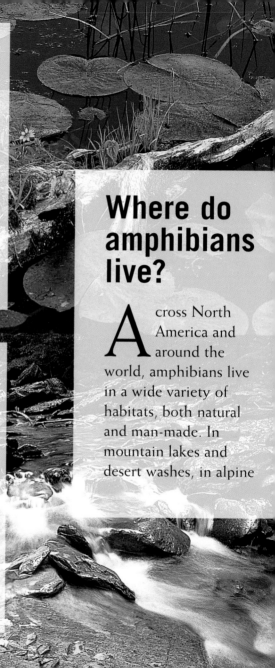

Where do amphibians live?

Across North
America and
around the
world, amphibians live
in a wide variety of
habitats, both natural
and man-made. In
mountain lakes and
desert washes, in alpine

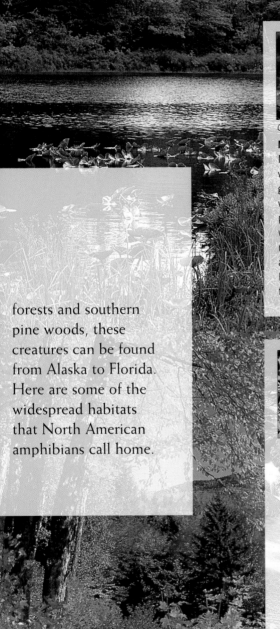

Carpenter Frog page 95

MARSHES AND BOGS

Marshes, filled with shallow water and vegetation, are great places to see frogs, which find food and hiding places here. Bogs are special wetlands with spongelike mosses, carnivorous plants, and such amphibians as the Four-toed Salamander and the Carpenter Frog.

forests and southern pine woods, these creatures can be found from Alaska to Florida. Here are some of the widespread habitats that North American amphibians call home.

Red Eft (immature Eastern Newt) page 146

WOODLANDS

Woodlands of all types span North America and are home to many amphibians. Western Toads inhabit Colorado's aspen forests, Red Efts scurry about in hardwood forests of New Hampshire, and Oak Toads live in dry pine and oak woodlands of South Carolina.

Eastern Tiger Salamander page 109

GRASSLANDS

Grasslands, plains, and brushlands may seem like strange areas to search for amphibians, but species such as the Eastern Tiger Salamander, Plains Spadefoot, and Western Chorus Frog are perfectly at home there.

MOUNTAINS

Mountains, depending on how high up they range, can hold great numbers of amphibians. In the East, the southern Appalachian Mountains are one of the best places in the world for salamanders, as the cool, moist climate is perfect for them. Western mountains are higher, and no amphibians live on high western peaks, but some, such as Mountain Treefrogs, can be found at lower elevations.

Yonahlossee Salamander page 136

Couch's Spadefoot page 59

DESERTS
Desert scrublands are a hot,
inhospitable amphibian environment
for much of the year, and their
amphibians spend most of their time
in the shade or underground. Red-
spotted Toads hunt for their prey after
sunset, and Couch's Spadefoot Toads
emerge from their burrows when
summer rains are heaviest.

CITIES AND SUBURBS
Cities and suburbs are the habitats of
most of the people in North America.
They also provide habitats for a great
many frogs, toads, and salamanders,
which live in parks, roadside ditches,
gardens, and greenhouses.

Woodhouse's Toad page 69

Ranges

An amphibian's range is the part of the country where it lives. When you learn about an amphibian's range, you must also look at its habitat. If its range is Kentucky and its habitat is mountain streams, that means it will be found only in parts of Kentucky that have mountain streams.

Great Smoky Mountains

IT'S NOT THE HEAT, IT'S THE HUMIDITY

High humidity throughout the year generally makes a region a good place for amphibians and amphibian watchers to prowl. The southeastern United States has a warm climate, lots of rainfall, and many good amphibian habitats, including mountain streams. This combination of things makes this region home to a long list of amphibian species. The United States overall has 211 species.

All of Canada: 39 species

- 60 + species
- 41–59 species
- 26–40 species
- 10–25 species
- 0–9 species

This map of North America shows the distribution of amphibians in different areas.

Northwestern Salamander (page 107)

TOO COLD

Alaska has only six species of amphibians: Northwestern Salamander, Long-toed Salamander, Roughskin Newt, Western Toad, Wood Frog, and Oregon Spotted Frog. Other places that have excessive cold, heat, and/or high elevations also have short amphibian lists. All of Canada has just 39 species.

THE BIG CHILL

North America went through several ice ages thousands of years ago. During these periods, huge glaciers (land-size masses of ice) covered large parts of the continent. Mountainous areas that were never covered by glaciers have a great number of species, especially salamanders, which flourish in forested hillsides and mountain valleys. The amphibians that developed in these regions over thousands and thousands of years were never killed off by the freezing, crushing ice of the glaciers. The southern Appalachian Mountains, including those in Great Smoky Mountains National Park in Tennessee and North Carolina have great numbers of salamanders.

Finding amphibians

Looking for amphibians is the best part of studying them. This is true whether you are a fourth grader or a college professor. There is nothing like the thrill of the search. Whether you are riding along an Arizona desert road during a summer monsoon rain, lifting stones beside an Arkansas creek, or searching out an Ontario springtime pool full of chorusing frogs, the possibilities are endless. Here are some of the basic strategies for making your amphibian prowls successful.

DAYTIME

Bring a pair of binoculars, if you have them. Watch along the edges and in the shallows of ponds and streams and in wet meadows for frogs and tadpoles.

Searching for amphibians in a beaver pond

NIGHTTIME

Nighttime is the right time for many salamanders and frogs. Get together with an adult and let people know where you are going. A flashlight is useful for a nighttime amphibian prowl, but a headlamp

A nighttime amphibian survey

leaves both of your hands free and always points in the right direction—where your eyes are looking. Check out the edges and shallows of ponds, streams, and wet meadows. Watch and listen for species moving about on land, in vegetation, and in and under the water. Keep your ears attuned for chorusing frogs.

BREEDING SEASONS

Visit springtime pools and other amphibian concentration areas during the breeding season and especially during the spring rains, when breeding species are on the move to pools. Many species of frogs and mole salamanders may be seen crossing back roads on rainy evenings. From Cape Cod to Colorado, during and just after periods of summer rains, watch for spadefoot toads and other summer breeding species.

Viewing Spotted Frog tadpoles

LOOKING HIGH AND LOW

Look in and around streams and under rocks, logs, and boards for salamanders and frogs. Watch along stream banks and in the shallowest, quietest water. Fast-flowing or deep water is harder to work in. At breeding pools of frogs and mole salamanders, look for egg masses. These are usually easy to spot.

43

Identifying amphibians

After you have found a great-looking frog or salamander, you will want to know exactly what species you are looking at. That will help you figure out which amphibians are most common in your area.

Ask questions

When you are trying to determine a species of amphibian, ask yourself a series of questions.

IS IT A FROG OR A SALAMANDER?

This is the first question to ask, and the answer is usually obvious.

Oak Toad page 70

Longtail Salamander page 118

HOW BIG IS IT?

Another good question, but remember that these creatures grow, and the one you are looking at may still be young.

WHAT IS THE HABITAT?

Some amphibians can live in many habitats, while some are very particular. Habitat is almost always a very good clue for narrowing down the species.

WHAT COLOR IS IT—ON BOTH ITS TOPSIDE AND UNDERSIDE?

Look at the colors carefully but remember that many species of amphibians have quite a range of color variation—and can also change color. Look for spots, stripes, and other patterns.

WHAT OTHER DETAILS CAN YOU SEE?

How many toes does it have and what do they look like? How long is its tail? Is the skin smooth or warty? These and other similar questions, when answered, will get you to the right species.

Spring Peeper page 84

WHAT ARE ITS CALLS?

Frogs and toads have characteristic calls. If you can learn them, it will be a big help in correctly identifying species, especially those that look similar.

WHAT IS THE RANGE?

No matter how much a certain toad or salamander looks like one in the book, if it is not recorded as living in your part of the country, you have to keep trying.

Amphibian conservation

Amphibians are one of the most diverse and remarkable groups of creatures on earth. They have inhabited the planet for millions of years. Of course, not every amphibian species that ever lived is still alive today.

Signs to protect the Yosemite Toad (page 63) breeding habitat

Danger!

Species of amphibians, as well as other animals and plants, evolve and thrive and then eventually become extinct. This is part of the natural order of life on earth. But there are also a number of unnatural events that are making life more and more difficult for amphibians every day. Huge numbers of amphibians are losing ground to environmental problems. Every amphibian in every corner of the world, even those many miles away from the nearest road or human settlement, is under attack. Conservationists and scientists are studying the plight of the amphibians. If we can understand the problems, we can work for answers.

LOSS OF HABITAT

This is one of the four major concerns for the future of amphibians. When people are cutting forests, filling wetlands, and carving up prairies, they do not think too much about the amphibians that live there. Many amphibians are literally running out of habitat.

Cheat Mountain Salamander, an endangered species

ULTRAVIOLET RADIATION
Herpetologists have found that the sun's ultraviolet radiation, the same rays that are harmful to humans, can cause many problems in amphibians, including a great number of body deformities.

*Wyoming Toad,
an endangered subspecies of Canadian Toad*

*Adult California
Red-legged Frog, an
endangered subspecies
of Red-legged Frog*

POLLUTION
This is another amphibian killer. Oil, toxic waste, and many other pollutants find their way into our waters, especially in settled areas. We have developed complicated and costly methods for making the water safe again for humans, but the ponds and meadows that frogs call home do not have filters on them.

WHAT CAN A KID DO?
Some people say that it will be up to your generation to save the world and its wonderful creatures and environments. That is too big a job for anyone. However, you can do your part for amphibians by thinking of them as living things that share space on this planet with us. Don't bother them or collect them or buy and sell them. Do study them and marvel at them and make as many people aware of them as you can. These efforts will go a long way toward helping amphibians.

ACID PRECIPITATION
Whether it is acid rain, fog, or snow, this type of precipitation—which contains acid that kills living things in lakes, ponds, and streams—is making life miserable for millions of amphibians the world over.

*California Red-legged
Frog tadpoles*

Using the field guide

This section features 50 common North American amphibians and includes brief descriptions of 87 more. Color photographs and details about each amphibian are included to help you identify it. Amphibians appearing on facing pages together are either related or share some traits or characteristics.

California Newt page 149

AMPHIBIAN I.D. TIPS

- Sometimes a single field mark, like a stripe down the back, is more important in identifying a species than a more complete description. The animal's color, for instance, may vary so much that it is not important.
- Stripes are lines that follow the amphibian's length (in the same direction as the backbone). Bands, bars, or rings circle around the body, like a belt.
- Blotches, or splotches, are bigger than spots and often odd-shaped.

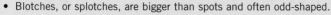

ICONS
These icons appear on each left-hand page in the field guide. They identify an amphibian's general shape and category.

 Frogs and Toads

 Salamanders

Green Treefrog page 80

SHAPE ICON
This icon identifies the featured amphibian's general shape and category.

NAME
Each amphibian's common and scientific names appear here.

BOX HEADING
The box heading alerts you to other amphibians covered in the box that are similar to the main amphibian on the page.

EASTERN NARROWMOUTH TOAD
Gastrophryne carolinensis

All narrowmouth toads spend a lot of their time underground, but if you look under boards and other ground debris, you are bound to find one eventually. When you do, you will see a strange-looking, pointed toad running to get out of sight. Often these toads can be spotted at night when they are prowling around looking for their favorite food—ants.

LOOK AND LISTEN FOR: A small, smooth-skinned toad with a pointed head and a fold of skin across its head behind its eyes; body is variably colored above, dark below. Call is a sheeplike "baaa."

SIZE: 1–1½".

HABITAT: Pond edges, under boards and vegetation, and in burrows.

RANGE: Southeastern U.S.

GREAT PLAINS NARROWMOUTH TOAD
Gastrophryne olivacea
LOOK AND LISTEN FOR: A small toad very similar to Eastern Narrowmouth Toad but olive to gray above and light below. Call is a "peep" followed by a high-pitched bleat. **SIZE:** 1–1½". **HABITAT:** A variety of moist areas, including under leaves and in burrows. **RANGE:** Southern Nebraska and south to Texas; also Arizona.

SHEEP FROG
Hypopachus variolosus
LOOK AND LISTEN FOR: A smooth-skinned, greenish-brown to brown narrowmouth toad. Has a pointed snout and fold of skin at back of neck. Yellow line down center of back. Call sounds like sheep bleating. **SIZE:** 1–1½". **HABITAT:** Edges of marshes and ponds, and other moist places. **RANGE:** Southern Texas.

50

IDENTIFICATION CAPSULE
The identification capsule covers all the details you need to identify an amphibian: color, pattern, size, shape, and other field marks discussed in this book.

RANGE AND HABITAT
The range and habitat listings tell you whether or not an amphibian is likely to be seen in your area.

CAUTION
The skin secretions (fluids) of many amphibians can cause itching or burning. If you handle an amphibian, never rub your eyes. Wash your hands as soon as you can.

EASTERN NARROWMOUTH TOAD
Gastrophryne carolinensis

All narrowmouth toads spend a lot of their time underground, but if you look under boards and other ground debris, you are bound to find one eventually. When you do, you will see a strange-looking, pointed toad running to get out of sight. Often these toads can be spotted at night when they are prowling around looking for their favorite food—ants.

LOOK AND LISTEN FOR: A small, smooth-skinned toad with a pointed head and a fold of skin across its head behind its eyes; body is variably

colored above, dark below. Call is
a sheeplike "baaa."

SIZE: 1–1½".

HABITAT: Pond edges, under boards
and vegetation, and in burrows.

RANGE: Southeastern U.S.

GREAT PLAINS NARROWMOUTH TOAD
Gastrophryne olivacea

LOOK AND LISTEN FOR: A small toad very similar
to Eastern Narrowmouth Toad but olive to
gray above and light below. Call is a
"peep" followed by a high-pitched bleat.
SIZE: 1–1½". **HABITAT:** A variety of moist
areas, including under leaves and in
burrows. **RANGE:** Southern Nebraska and
south to Texas; also Arizona.

SHEEP FROG
Hypopachus variolosus

LOOK AND LISTEN FOR: A smooth-skinned,
greenish-brown to brown narrowmouth
toad. Has a pointed snout and fold of skin
at back of neck. Yellow line down center
of back. Call sounds like sheep bleating.
SIZE: 1–1¾". **HABITAT:** Edges of marshes and
ponds, and other moist places. **RANGE:**
Southern Texas.

CLIFF CHIRPING FROG
Eleutherodactylus marnockii

When you spend your life scrambling about on cliffs and ledges, webbed feet get in the way. Chirping frogs are the only North American frogs that have no webbing between their toes. They are very good rock climbers and their flat bodies let them slip easily into small cracks if danger approaches.

LOOK AND LISTEN FOR: A small, greenish and brown frog with a flattened body and rather large head. Call is given throughout the year and

RIO GRANDE CHIRPING FROG
Eleutherodactylus cystignathoides

LOOK AND LISTEN FOR: A small, mostly grayish to brownish frog with dark flecks on its upper sides. Call is cricketlike and given irregularly. Very common within its range and easy to find under boards and on watered lawns. **SIZE:** ¾–1". **HABITAT:** Gardens, lawns, ditches, and leaf litter. **RANGE:** Southernmost Texas.

SPOTTED CHIRPING FROG
Eleutherodactylus guttilatus

LOOK AND LISTEN FOR: A small, flat, greenish frog with brown markings. Toes squared off. Call resembles trill of cricket. **SIZE:** 1–1½". **HABITAT:** Caves and cracks in limestone hills. **RANGE:** Big Bend National Park and surrounding area in Texas.

sounds like cricket chirps.

SIZE: 1–1¼".

HABITAT: Eastern and southern cliff faces.

RANGE: Central Texas.

53

GREENHOUSE FROG
Eleutherodactylus planirostris

Most North American frogs and toads are natives, but this little fellow was brought to Florida from the Caribbean islands. It is now very common—in fact, it may be the most commonly seen frog in some areas. Greenhouse Frogs like greenhouses, of course, but they also like lawns, especially when a sprinkler is going.

LOOK AND LISTEN FOR: A small, reddish-brown frog with dark blotches or 2 light stripes on its back. Call is

BARKING FROG
Eleutherodactylus augusti

LOOK AND LISTEN FOR: A plump, brownish frog with dark skin blotches and a fold on each side and behind the head. Call sounds like a dog bark, given irregularly. **SIZE:** 2–3¾".
HABITAT: Caves and cracks in limestone hills.
RANGE: Southeastern Arizona; southeastern New Mexico east to central Texas.

WHITE-LIPPED FROG
Leptodactylus labialis

LOOK AND LISTEN FOR: A brown to gray frog with dark skin blotches and a white line along its upper lip. Call is repeated constantly and sounds like "throw-up, throw-up, throw-up." Yuck! Mostly active at night. **SIZE:** 1½–2". **HABITAT:** Moist fields and grasslands. **RANGE:** Southernmost Texas.

a faint "peep" given a few times in a row.
SIZE: 1–1½".
HABITAT: Almost anywhere on land.
RANGE: Florida.

TAILED FROG
Ascaphus truei

TADPOLE

This unique frog lives in clear, cold mountain streams, where its tadpoles hold on to rocks with a suction-cup-like mouth. The Tailed Frog gets its name from the projection at the end of the male's body. It looks like a short tail but is actually used in mating. Tailed Frogs, along with a few species in New Zealand, are the most primitive frogs in the world. This means that they are still very similar to early frogs on earth.

LOOK AND LISTEN FOR: A variably colored frog (reddish-brown to olive to gray) with a light area outlined in black on the top of its snout; skin is smooth but has numerous warts; male has a "tail." Apparently voiceless.

SIZE: 1–2".

HABITAT: Cold, fast-flowing mountain streams.

RANGE: Southern British Columbia to northern California; also western Montana to Idaho.

EASTERN SPADEFOOT
Scaphiopus holbrookii

Spadefoot toads are very interesting to look at, with their big eyes and vertical, catlike pupils. They are also fun to listen to, with their weird, nasal calls. But if you want to find them, you have to pay attention to the weather and get an umbrella. Spadefoots spend much of their time underground, but during a heavy rain they all gather at their breeding pools and call loudly and often.

LOOK AND LISTEN FOR: A brown to blackish toad with bulging eyes (and vertical pupils) and a light line running down its back behind each eye; hind feet have a "spade" for digging. Call is a very nasal and explosive "kwonk" repeated frequently.

SIZE: 2–3".

HABITAT: Forested areas.

RANGE: Oklahoma to Massachusetts and south.

COUCH'S SPADEFOOT
Scaphiopus couchii

LOOK AND LISTEN FOR: A yellowish to greenish toad with variable amounts of dark blotching, eyes with vertical pupils, and a "spade" on each hind foot. Call sounds like a lamb bleating. **SIZE:** 2½–3½".
HABITAT: Desert scrublands, dry plains, grasslands, and semi-desert areas. **RANGE:** Southwestern U.S.

PLAINS SPADEFOOT
Spea bombifrons

In sandy grasslands of the Great Plains, this spadefoot toad, which has the profile of a miniature bulldog, can be quite abundant. Spadefoot toads of all kinds are easily overlooked, as they are often underground. The "spades" on their hind feet act like little shovels and allow them to dig quickly into the loose soil they prefer.

LOOK AND LISTEN FOR: A spadefoot toad with light gray to brown skin, orange- or yellow-tipped warts on its back, and a bony knob

GREAT BASIN SPADEFOOT
Spea intermontana

LOOK AND LISTEN FOR: A grayish-green spadefoot toad with a low knob between its eyes. Call is rapidly repeated raspy notes. **SIZE:** 1½–2½". **HABITAT:** Varies, from coniferous (trees with cones) forests to sage grasslands. **RANGE:** Southern British Columbia to central California and east to Rockies.

WESTERN SPADEFOOT
Spea hammondii

LOOK AND LISTEN FOR: A gray, brown, or greenish spadefoot toad with no knob between its eyes. Call is raspy snoring notes. **SIZE:** 1½–2½". **HABITAT:** River floodplains, grasslands, and dry lands. **RANGE:** Southwestern U.S. and western California. **CAUTION:** If handled, secretes fluid that can cause itching.

between its eyes; the "spade" on its hind feet is wedge-shaped. Call is a raspy bleat or short trill.

SIZE: 1½–2½".

HABITAT: Dry grasslands.

RANGE: Alberta to Manitoba and south through Great Plains.

61

WESTERN TOAD
Bufo boreas

The Western Toad is typical of many species in the true toad family—plump and warty and found on land much of the year. Like many toads, the females lay tremendous numbers of eggs—about 12,000—in two long strands in the water. This is the only true toad through much of the Northwest and it is active even when temperatures are as low as 40 degrees Fahrenheit.

LOOK AND LISTEN FOR: A blackish to greenish toad with a light line down the middle of its back. Call is light peeping chirps; this toad has no vocal sac.

EGGS

Size: 2½–5".

Habitat: Moist areas from grasslands to woodlands.

Range: Alaska to Alberta and south to California, Utah, and Colorado.

Caution: All toads have poison glands. Wash your hands after touching any toad.

GREAT PLAINS TOAD
Bufo cognatus

Look and listen for: A grayish to greenish toad with dark olive to brown blotches (with light borders) on its upperparts; V-shaped crest behind each eye. Call is a very loud, high-pitched clatter lasting 5 to 50 seconds; oval vocal sac. **Size:** 2–4½". **Habitat:** Grasslands and brushlands. **Range:** Great Plains from southern Alberta and south; southwestern U.S.

YOSEMITE TOAD
Bufo canorus

Look and listen for: A medium-size toad. Both males and females are yellow-olive above; male has small dark flecks, female and young have large dark blotches. Call is a pleasant trill. **Size:** 2–3". **Habitat:** Meadows and woodland clearings in mountains. **Range:** Sierra Nevada and southern California mountains.

63

RED-SPOTTED TOAD
Bufo punctatus

At the twilight hour, when the red glow is fading from the western sky, watch for Red-spotted Toads climbing up onto rocks and boulders at the edges of a pond or spring. Here they begin their nightly activities, which include calling and feeding. These rock-climbing toads have flattish bodies that help them squeeze into and under crevices.

LOOK AND LISTEN FOR: A gray, reddish-brown, or olive-colored toad with a flat body, pointed snout, and warts with reddish tips. Call is a high-pitched trill.

SIZE: 1½–3".

HABITAT: Rocky areas in deserts and canyons; also grasslands.

RANGE: Southwestern U.S.

ARIZONA TOAD
Bufo microscaphus

LOOK AND LISTEN FOR: A variably colored (greenish to pinkish) toad with a light band crossing the top of its head, including the eyelids. Call is a pleasant trill of 10 seconds or less. **SIZE:** 2–3¼". **HABITAT:** Streambeds and washes in semi-dry areas. **RANGE:** Southwestern U.S. (many separated populations).

SONORAN GREEN TOAD
Bufo retiformis

LOOK AND LISTEN FOR: A striking, black-backed toad with yellowish-green blotches on its upper sides. Call is a short buzzy trill. **SIZE:** 1½–2¼". **HABITAT:** Dry grasslands and shrublands. **RANGE:** South-central Arizona.

65

TEXAS TOAD
Bufo speciosus

During the evening after a good soaking rain, between April and September, Texas Toads will march across the damp, southwestern plains to small pools and water holes looking for mates. One of these pools of water can turn into a swarming mass of Texas Toads in just a few hours.

LOOK AND LISTEN FOR: A uniformly colored, greenish to brownish, plump toad with small warts. Call is a very short, high-pitched trill repeated frequently; oval vocal sac.

GREEN TOAD
Bufo debilis

LOOK AND LISTEN FOR: A yellow-green to green, flat-bodied toad with many dark flecks on its upper sides. Call is a weak, buzzing trill of 10 seconds or less. **SIZE:** 1¼–2". **HABITAT:** Dry plains, grasslands, and foothills. **RANGE:** Southern Colorado and Kansas, south to Arizona and Texas.

HOUSTON TOAD
Bufo houstonensis

LOOK AND LISTEN FOR: A gray-brown, plump toad, often with a light stripe down the middle of its back. Male has dark throat. Call is high-pitched trill. This is an endangered species. **SIZE:** 2–3½". **HABITAT:** Pinewoods and coastal prairies. **RANGE:** Southeastern Texas.

SIZE: 2–3¼".

HABITAT: Short-grass plains with mesquite (thorny trees).

RANGE: Texas; parts of Oklahoma, Kansas, and New Mexico.

67

AMERICAN TOAD
Bufo americanus

LOOK AND LISTEN FOR: A plump, brown, gray, or reddish toad with a round snout, prominent warts, and often a light line down the center of its back. Call is a trill of up to 30 seconds.

SIZE: 2–4".

HABITAT: Varied, including gardens, woodlands, ponds, and lakes.

RANGE: Eastern Canada and U.S., except in southeastern lowlands.

Wilderness areas, city parks, and most habitats in between are home to the familiar American Toad. Depending on location, these toads breed from February to July. Their trills, given both day and night, will lead you to them. American Toads are easily approached and watched when trilling. As with other toads, handling them will not give you warts. This helpful toad eats lots of insects.

WOODHOUSE'S TOAD
Bufo woodhousii

LOOK AND LISTEN FOR: A plump, brown, gray, or greenish toad with a light line down the center of its back. Resembles American Toad but has a more pointed snout and often has prominent dark blotches on its back. Call sounds like "waaaaah" and lasts 1 to 3 seconds. **SIZE:** 2½–4½". **HABITAT:** Varied, from river bottoms to mountain canyons. **RANGE:** Widespread in U.S.; separated populations in far West.

CANADIAN TOAD
Bufo hemiophrys

LOOK AND LISTEN FOR: A variably colored (usually brown, gray, or greenish) toad with a light line down the center of its back and a prominent bony hump between its eyes. Call is a short, weak trill given 2 to 3 times per minute. **SIZE:** 2–3". **HABITAT:** Edges of ponds, marshes, and streams in prairies. **RANGE:** Alberta, Saskatchewan, and Manitoba, south into north-central U.S.

69

OAK TOAD
Bufo quercicus

E very amphibian has its favorite hours of activity, and many amphibians are most active at night, when it is safer for them to roam around. The Oak Toad, however, is most often seen during daylight hours. This is the smallest North American toad.

Watch for it rummaging around in ground litter and debris.

LOOK AND LISTEN FOR: A very small gray to blackish toad with a prominent white to yellowish stripe down the center of its back and red warts on the undersides of

SOUTHERN TOAD
Bufo terrestris

LOOK AND LISTEN FOR: A brown to reddish or blackish toad with prominent knobby head crests. Call is similar to American Toad's but higher pitched and shorter. **SIZE:** 1¾–4". **HABITAT:** Variety of lowland habitats; sandy soils preferred. **RANGE:** Southeastern U.S.

GULF COAST TOAD
Bufo valliceps

LOOK AND LISTEN FOR: A light brown to blackish, somewhat flat toad with a prominent, light-edged dark band on each side of its body. Call is a short trill repeated several times, with a few seconds between trills. **SIZE:** 2–4½". **HABITAT:** Varied, including grasslands, beaches, and roadside ditches. **RANGE:** Texas to Mississippi.

its feet. Pictured here with vocal sac extended. Call sounds like the "peep" of a baby bird.

SIZE: ¾–1¼".

HABITAT: Lowland pine and oak forests.

RANGE: Southeastern U.S.

71

CANE TOAD
Bufo marinus

Wherever the Cane Toad is introduced, whether to Florida or Australia or somewhere else, it becomes a nuisance within a short time. It breeds year-round and its populations can get enormous very quickly. Speaking of enormous, this is the largest toad and can weigh up to 4 pounds.

One of the biggest ever found in the United States was nicknamed Jabba the Toad, after the *Star Wars* ® character. Cane Toads are active mostly at night.

LOOK AND LISTEN FOR: An enormous yellow-brown to brown toad with a huge poison gland behind each ear.

SIZE: 4–9".

HABITAT: Suburban gardens and yards and other humid areas.

RANGE: Southernmost Texas and southeastern Florida (introduced to both places).

CAUTION: Poisons may burn hands and eyes.

COLORADO RIVER TOAD
Bufo alvarius

LOOK AND LISTEN FOR: The largest native toad in the U.S., its body is olive, grayish, or brown with mostly smooth skin and 1 or 2 white warts near the corners of its mouth. Call is a honk or toot lasting ½ to 1 second. **SIZE:** 3–7". **HABITAT:** Deserts, usually close to wet areas. **RANGE:** Southern and western Arizona and nearby California and New Mexico.

MEXICAN BURROWING TOAD
Rhinophrynus dorsalis

LOOK AND LISTEN FOR: A round, dark, bizarre-looking toad with a pointed head and a prominent yellow to red stripe down the middle of its back. Call is a deep, moaning "whooa." **SIZE:** 2–2¾". **HABITAT:** Woodlands and fields with loose soil. **RANGE:** Southernmost Texas.

NORTHERN CRICKET FROG
Acris crepitans

Cricket frogs are non-climbing treefrogs with no pads on their toes. Like many frogs, Northern Cricket Frogs can be quite differently colored from frog to frog. They are one of the last frogs to breed in spring and early summer. Even though they may be abundant and active during the day, their small size can make them a challenge to find.

SOUTHERN CRICKET FROG
Acris gryllus

LOOK AND LISTEN FOR: A small frog very similar to the Northern Cricket Frog, with a dark triangle between its eyes, a pattern of darker stripes and blotches, and the same highly variable colors. Call is a rapidly repeated clicking. **SIZE:** ¾–1¼". **HABITAT:** Grassy edges of ponds, streams, and ditches in lowlands. **RANGE:** Southeastern U.S.

LOOK AND LISTEN FOR: A small, variably colored frog with warty skin and a dark triangular mark between its eyes; upperparts have dark blotches and/or stripes. Call sounds like 2 pebbles being tapped together rapidly.

SIZE: ½–1½".

HABITAT: Grassy edges of ponds and streams.

RANGE: Most of eastern U.S.

75

PACIFIC TREEFROG
Hyla regilla

Not everyone has heard of the Pacific Treefrog, but everyone knows what these creatures say: "ribbit, ribbit." Because moviemakers have put the sound of this common California treefrog into so many film soundtracks, people think that lots of frogs say "ribbit," but only this one does. This tiny frog is found from the coast to mountains 10,000 feet high.

LOOK AND LISTEN FOR: A highly variably colored (often green or brown) treefrog with a dark line through its eyes. Usually found on or close to the ground. Call is the well-known "ribbit, ribbit."

SIZE: ¾–2".

HABITAT: Varied, from grasslands to deserts to forests.

RANGE: British Columbia and south to California and Nevada.

CANYON TREEFROG
Hyla arenicolor

LOOK AND LISTEN FOR: A warty, olive-gray to brown treefrog with no dark stripe through its eyes, with or without dark blotches on its upperparts. Call is an explosive buzzing whirr lasting 1 to 3 seconds. **SIZE:** 1¼–2¼". **HABITAT:** Streams and streambeds in grasslands and dry woodlands. **RANGE:** Southwestern U.S.

CALIFORNIA TREEFROG
Hyla cadaverina

LOOK AND LISTEN FOR: A warty, grayish treefrog, usually with round, dark blotches on its skin. Call is an often-repeated quack. **SIZE:** 1–2". **HABITAT:** Varied, from desert canyons to mountain pine forests, near streams. **RANGE:** Southwestern California.

GRAY TREEFROG
Hyla versicolor

There are actually two gray treefrogs—the Gray Treefrog and the Cope's Gray Treefrog (*Hyla chrysoscelis*). They look so much alike that only an expert can tell them apart—and then only by their calls! In spring and summer, listen for their sweet nighttime trills coming from bushes and trees. Sometimes these and other treefrogs come to windows and lights searching for insects to eat.

LOOK AND LISTEN FOR: A warty, brown to green to gray treefrog, with a dark-edged light spot below each eye and usually a few dark

PINE BARRENS TREEFROG
Hyla andersonii

LOOK AND LISTEN FOR: A smooth, green treefrog with a bold, white-edged purple stripe on its sides and legs. Call is a low honking, repeated once a second, 20 or more times in a row. This frog is an endangered species that should never be disturbed. **SIZE:** 1–2". **HABITAT:** Bogs and swamps in pine woods. **RANGE:** New Jersey and south to Texas in small, separated populations.

BIRD-VOICED TREEFROG
Hyla avivoca

LOOK AND LISTEN FOR: A greenish, grayish, or brownish treefrog, quite similar to the gray treefrogs, with a white spot below its eye and blotches on its back. Call is very different—a lovely, birdlike twittering, given from shrubs. **SIZE:** 1–2". **HABITAT:** Swamps bordering rivers and streams. **RANGE:** Southern Illinois to Louisiana and Florida; Georgia and South Carolina.

blotches on its back. Calls of both species are trills; Cope's is faster.

SIZE: 1¼–2¼".

HABITAT: Woodland shrubs and trees near water.

RANGE: Eastern U.S. and southernmost Canada.

GREEN TREEFROG
Hyla cinerea

Whether you are searching for them among
cattail reeds in the daytime or on a wall near
an outside light at night, you are bound to be
delighted with Green Treefrogs when you find them.
When Green Treefrogs get together at mating sites
they may number in the thousands.

LOOK AND LISTEN FOR: A long-legged, green treefrog with polished, smooth skin and usually a bold white stripe down each side of its body. Call resembles a cowbell clinking about once a second.

SIZE: 1¼–2¼".

HABITAT: Vegetation, usually along edges of streams, marshes, and ponds.

RANGE: Southeastern U.S.

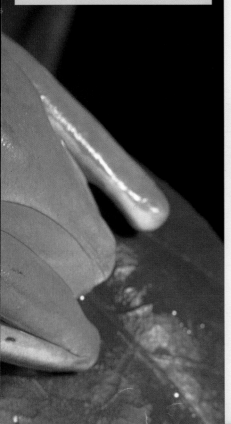

SQUIRREL TREEFROG
Hyla squirella

LOOK AND LISTEN FOR: A variably marked, common treefrog. May be green to brown, plain or with spots, and with or without a white stripe along its lower lip and side of body. Calls include a nasal trill and grating quack. **SIZE:** 1–1½". **HABITAT:** Moist areas with trees; suburban homes. **RANGE:** Southeastern Virginia to Texas, mostly on coastal plain.

PINE WOODS TREEFROG
Hyla femoralis

LOOK AND LISTEN FOR: A smooth-skinned treefrog, usually brownish with darker skin blotches, but may be greenish or grayish. Call is a slow, rhythmic trill. **SIZE:** 1–1½". **HABITAT:** Pine woods, especially near swamps and other wet areas in lowlands. **RANGE:** Southeastern U.S.

81

BARKING TREEFROG
Hyla gratiosa

SPOTTED FORM

When spring rains fall, Barking Treefrogs come down from the trees and make their way to their breeding ponds.

LOOK AND LISTEN FOR: A green, gray, or brownish treefrog with grainy (not smooth) skin, a light line along its side, and upper sides with or without round dark blotches. Call on land is like a dog's bark; in water, call is "took."

SIZE: 2–2¾".

HABITAT: Sandy areas near ponds and streams in lowlands.

RANGE: Southeastern U.S.

CUBAN TREEFROG
Ostepilus septentrionalis

LOOK AND LISTEN FOR: A green to gray treefrog with warty skin and huge toe pads. Call is raspy, like that of the Southern Leopard Frog. The largest North American treefrog, it can swallow a large variety of prey, including many other smaller, native frogs. **SIZE:** 2–5". **HABITAT:** Moist, shady areas; suburban homes. **RANGE:** Southern Florida.

MOUNTAIN TREEFROG
Hyla eximia

LOOK AND LISTEN FOR: A green treefrog with a purple stripe along its side from snout to hind leg. Sometimes has other purple bars on lower back. Call is a series of low-pitched notes. **SIZE:** 1–2". **HABITAT:** Mountain meadows and edges of pools and slow streams. **RANGE:** Central Arizona to western New Mexico.

SPRING PEEPER
Pseudacris crucifer

One of the first true signs of spring in New England and nearby areas is the evening calling of the Spring Peepers. Snow may linger in the darker parts of the woods, but the ponds, free from ice, attract these handsome little frogs with their spring choruses. The residents of Martha's Vineyard, Massachusetts, call these creatures Pinkletinks.

LOOK AND LISTEN FOR: A small, light to dark brown frog with an X-shaped dark mark on its back. Call is a "peep" or "preep" in a short trill, given once a second.

SIZE: ¾–1½".

HABITAT: Ponds and swamps in woodlands.

RANGE: Eastern Canada and U.S.

SPOTTED CHORUS FROG
Pseudacris clarkii

LOOK AND LISTEN FOR: A slender, gray to olive-gray chorus frog with a green triangle between its eyes and green spots on its uppersides. **SIZE:** ¾–1¼". **HABITAT:** Prairies. **RANGE:** Kansas and south to Texas.

WESTERN CHORUS FROG
Pseudacris triseriata

LOOK AND LISTEN FOR: The northernmost and westernmost chorus frog. Brown to greenish with 3 darker stripes or rows of spots on its upper sides. Call is "crreek-crreek-crreek." **SIZE:** ¾–1½". **HABITAT:** Wet meadows, grasslands, and woodlands. **RANGE:** Northwestern Canada, much of eastern half of U.S.

85

ORNATE CHORUS FROG
Pseudacris ornata

Chorus frogs, cricket frogs, and other members of the treefrog family can be very common over wide areas, but still they are not well known. This is because of their size. Many of the most remarkable American frogs and toads, including this beautiful frog, are small. Think small and you will find a lot more frogs! This species spends most of its time in a burrow.

LOOK AND LISTEN FOR: A chorus frog with highly variable colors that has a dark mask through its eyes and light-rimmed dark spots

along its sides. Call is a high-pitched "peep" given about once a second.

SIZE: 1–1½".

HABITAT: Ponds, ditches, and wet meadows.

RANGE: Southeastern U.S.

SOUTHERN CHORUS FROG
Pseudacris nigrita

LOOK AND LISTEN FOR: A slim, light gray to light brown chorus frog with bold black markings in 3 rows on its back and a black line through its eyes. Call is an unmusical trill. **SIZE:** ¾–1¼". **HABITAT:** Wet meadows, moist woodlands, ponds, and ditches. **RANGE:** Southeastern U.S.

LITTLE GRASS FROG
Pseudacris ocularis

LOOK AND LISTEN FOR: The smallest North American frog. Skin color varies a lot, but its tiny size and a dark line through its eyes are constants. Call is a series of weak, high-pitched chirps. **SIZE:** ½–⅝". **HABITAT:** Grassy edges of ponds, ditches, and cypress bays. **RANGE:** Southeastern U.S.

RED-LEGGED FROG
Rana aurora

Listen closely or you may miss the calls of the Red-legged Frog. Although it can grow to an impressive size, this handsome frog has weak call notes. On top of that, it likes to call while underwater, and then the notes are even harder to hear. Its short spring breeding season lasts one to two weeks. This frog is endangered.

LOOK AND LISTEN FOR: A gray to reddish-brown frog with 2 distinct ridges down its back. Yellowish

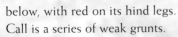

below, with red on its hind legs. Call is a series of weak grunts.

SIZE: 2–5".

HABITAT: Ponds with vegetation; also moist woods.

RANGE: Southern British Columbia and far western U.S.

FOOTHILL YELLOW-LEGGED FROG
Rana boylii

LOOK AND LISTEN FOR: A variably colored aquatic frog with a light triangle on top of its snout; hind legs have yellow undersides. Call is raspy and seldom heard. **SIZE:** 1½–3". **HABITAT:** Streams and rivers in chaparral (dense shrubs) and forests. **RANGE:** Oregon and California.

MOUNTAIN YELLOW-LEGGED FROG
Rana muscosa

LOOK AND LISTEN FOR: A dark frog with mottled greenish-black markings and a light stripe on its upper lip; below, hindlegs and belly are yellow. This is the only frog high up in the Sierra Nevada mountains. **SIZE:** 2–3¼". **HABITAT:** Banks of lakes, ponds, and streams. **RANGE:** Sierra Nevada and southern California mountains.

89

OREGON SPOTTED FROG
Rana pretiosa

Oregon Spotted Frogs, which have a pretty large range in the West, used to be much more common before Bullfrogs were introduced into the region. Bullfrogs have big bodies and big appetites and they like the taste of Oregon Spotted Frogs so much that in some places they have eaten this smaller species into extinction.

CASCADES FROG
Rana cascadae

LOOK AND LISTEN FOR: An olive-brown to brown frog with sharp-edged black spots on its back, a dark mask behind its eyes, and a light upper lip. Call is a series of slow croaks. **SIZE:** 1¾–2¼". **HABITAT:** Wet meadows and pond edges in mountains. **RANGE:** Olympic and Cascade mountains, from Washington to northern California.

LOOK AND LISTEN FOR: A brownish frog with dark spots on its back and a light stripe on its upper lip. Call is a short series of deep but weak notes.

SIZE: 2–4".

HABITAT: Marshy edges of cold lakes and streams.

RANGE: Southeastern Alaska and south to Nevada and Utah.

WOOD FROG
Rana sylvatica

Found north of the Arctic Circle, this is the northernmost amphibian in North America. Even before the last ice is melted from the edges of small ponds and pools in spring, Wood Frogs are quacking out their ducklike calls.

Outside the breeding season, these masked frogs will wander far from water.

LOOK AND LISTEN FOR: A light to dark brown frog with a dark mask and a light line on its upper lip. Call is a series of quacking notes.

SIZE: 1½–3¼".

HABITAT: Woods in East, tundra (treeless plains) in North, grasslands in West.

RANGE: Canada, Alaska, and south into eastern and northern U.S.

MINK FROG
Rana septentrionalis

LOOK AND LISTEN FOR: A brown to green frog of northern areas. Its back is solid or has many blackish patches; its lower jaw is bright green. Smells bad when handled. Call is a low-pitched croak. **SIZE:** 1¾–3". **HABITAT:** Ponds with lily pads; pond and marsh edges. **RANGE:** Manitoba and northeast to Labrador.

NORTHERN LEOPARD FROG
Rana pipiens

LOOK AND LISTEN FOR: A green or brown frog with bold, white-edged dark patches on its upper sides and distinct back ridges. Call is a combination of snoring and clucking notes. **SIZE:** 2–5". **HABITAT:** Wet meadows and grasslands; pond and marsh edges. **RANGE:** Eastern Canada and northern U.S.

FLORIDA LEOPARD FROG
Rana sphenocephala

Leopard frogs, including the widespread Florida Leopard Frog, are very good leapers and not easy to catch, but that doesn't stop people from trying. Many of these frogs are caught by fishermen, who use them as bait. They like wet grassy areas and can be very common if conditions are right.

LOOK AND LISTEN FOR: The most common big southeastern frog. Brown or green with numerous dark spots and distinct ridges on its back, and a white spot on its

eardrum. Call is a series of chuckling croaks.

SIZE: 2–3½".

HABITAT: Vegetation in and around any freshwater environment.

RANGE: Southeastern U.S.

PICKEREL FROG
Rana palustris

LOOK AND LISTEN FOR: A frog that resembles a leopard frog but is browner, with large, rectangular (not roundish) spots on its back; yellow or orange below and on undersides of thighs. Call is a 1- to 2-second snore. **SIZE:** 1¾–3½". **HABITAT:** Wet meadows, swamps, and streams. **RANGE:** Southeastern Canada and eastern U.S. **CAUTION:** Skin secretions may be irritating.

CARPENTER FROG
Rana virgatipes

LOOK AND LISTEN FOR: A brown frog with 4 obvious yellow stripes down its back. Call is likened to the sound of hammering: "ca-took, ca-took, ca-took". **SIZE:** 1½–2½". **HABITAT:** Coastal plain bogs and ponds. **RANGE:** New Jersey and south to South Carolina.

BULLFROG
Rana catesbeiana

Perhaps the most recognized amphibian on the continent, the Bullfrog is, among other things, an awesome predator. In its watery home it will eat other frogs and amphibians, fishes, small snakes, and even small songbirds and baby ducks—if it has the chance.

LOOK AND LISTEN FOR: The largest North American frog. Skin is plain green or patterned with dark markings above (darker in the Southeast). Call is the familiar, deep "jug-o'-rum."

SIZE: 4–8".

HABITAT: Quiet or slow-moving water with dense vegetation preferred.

RANGE: Eastern North America (introduced widely in western U.S. and Hawaii).

GREEN FROG
Rana clamitans

LOOK AND LISTEN FOR: A green to brownish frog often mistaken for larger Bullfrog. This species has a ridge running down each side of its back. Call is usually a single note and sounds like the plunk of a loose banjo string. **SIZE:** 2–3½". **HABITAT:** Shallow fresh water, including brooks, springs, and ponds. **RANGE:** Southeastern Canada and eastern U.S.

PIG FROG
Rana grylio

LOOK AND LISTEN FOR: Olive to brownish frog often mistaken for Bullfrog. This species has a pointed snout, dark spotting above, and fully webbed hind feet. Call is a piglike grunt. **SIZE:** 3½–5¼". **HABITAT:** Shallow ponds with lily pads; flooded fields and meadows. **RANGE:** South Carolina to eastern Texas.

MUDPUPPY
Necturus maculosus

Along the bottoms of lakes and streams, in places where rocks and logs are piled together, the Mudpuppy wanders in search of crayfishes and other aquatic—water-dwelling—creatures for food. Active at night and even in winter, when they move to deeper water, Mudpuppies are an impressive sight and worthy of a special search.

LOOK FOR: A very large, brown to grayish, aquatic salamander with dark spots on its back and sides.

Gills obvious.

SIZE: 8–17".

HABITAT: Strictly aquatic: rivers, lakes, and streams.

RANGE: Eastern U.S. and southeastern Canada.

DWARF WATERDOG
Necturus punctatus

LOOK FOR: A gilled, aquatic salamander similar to the Mudpuppy but much smaller and usually unspotted; brown above, whitish below. Waterdogs belong to the mudpuppy family. **SIZE:** 4½–7". **HABITAT:** Slow-moving streams with muddy or sandy bottoms. **RANGE:** Southeastern Virginia to Georgia.

GULF COAST WATERDOG
Necturus beyeri

LOOK FOR: A brown waterdog with many darker brown spots and blotches above; below, belly has many small dark spots. Gills prominent. **SIZE:** 6–8½". **HABITAT:** Spring-fed streams. **RANGE:** Texas to Mississippi.

HELLBENDER
Cryptobranchus alleganiensis

Fishermen casting out in the big, fast-flowing streams where Hellbenders live sometimes lure this gigantic, scary-looking amphibian out from under its rock shelters. Many people fear the Hellbender and say it is poisonous. Actually, it is harmless. The Hellbender is one of the largest salamanders in the world.

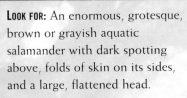

LOOK FOR: An enormous, grotesque, brown or grayish aquatic salamander with dark spotting above, folds of skin on its sides, and a large, flattened head.

SIZE: 12–30".

HABITAT: Under rocks and debris in rivers and large streams.

RANGE: New York and southwest to Missouri.

GREATER SIREN
Siren lacertina

Sirens have no hind legs. This fact and some other features of sirens make some scientists think they are not salamanders at all, but amphibians set apart from all others. Whatever they may be, sirens certainly are different. They will often give out a scream or howl if they are caught.

LOOK FOR: A very large, gray to olive, eel-like salamander with external gills and tiny front feet (no back feet). Body darker on top of back; sides with numerous small

LESSER SIREN
Siren intermedia

LOOK FOR: A large to very large, gray-brown to blackish, eel-like salamander. Similar to the Greater Siren but has a pointed tail and may be dark-spotted above. **SIZE:** 7–27". **HABITAT:** Muddy-bottomed ponds, streams, and ditches. **RANGE:** From Mississippi south to Texas, east around Gulf States, and north to North Carolina.

DWARF SIREN
Pseudobranchus striatus

LOOK FOR: A small, slender siren. Body brown above with yellow stripes on top and sides; greenish below with tiny yellow spots; 3 toes on each foot. **SIZE:** 4–6". **HABITAT:** Mud and vegetation in swamps, ponds, and marshes. **RANGE:** Southern South Carolina to Florida.

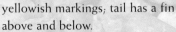

yellowish markings; tail has a fin above and below.

SIZE: 20–35".

HABITAT: Shallow bodies of water with abundant vegetation and muddy bottoms.

RANGE: Southeastern U.S.

TWO-TOED AMPHIUMA
Amphiuma means

THREE-TOED AMPHIUMA
Amphiuma tridactylum

LOOK FOR: An amphiuma very similar to the Two-toed, with 4 tiny legs, but each foot has 3 toes. **SIZE:** 18–36". **HABITAT:** Muddy-bottomed ponds, ditches, and bayous. **RANGE:** Lower Mississippi valley, from eastern Texas to Alabama.

Look for amphiumas in waters with lots of vegetation—especially at night when they are out feeding. Be careful if you intend to grab one. It is likely to bite you—and amphiumas can really bite!

LOOK FOR: The largest salamander in North America. Eellike body is dark brown to blackish (gray below), with 2 pairs of tiny legs and 2 toes per foot.

SIZE: 18–45".

HABITAT: Ponds, ditches, streams, and other freshwater habitats in lowlands.

RANGE: Southeastern U.S.

CAUTION: Bites if picked up.

CALIFORNIA GIANT SALAMANDER
Dicamptodon ensatus

This species, like others in the mole salamander family, spends most of its adult life underground. The adults are active and will bite and twist their bodies around if handled. The gilled, fin-tailed larvae are seen much more often. Lift rocks at the water's edge to find them.

LOOK FOR: A large, big-headed, brown salamander with black splotches above; whitish to light brown below.

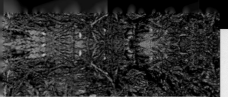

SIZE: 7–11".

HABITAT: Clear, cold streams and ponds and surrounding moist forests.

RANGE: Southern British Columbia and northwestern U.S.

LONG-TOED SALAMANDER
Ambystoma macrodactylum

LOOK FOR: A black salamander with long toes and a green to yellowish, solid or splotchy stripe on its back. SIZE: 4–6". HABITAT: Extremely varied, from sagelands to mountain lakes and alpine meadows. RANGE: Southeastern Alaska and south to northwestern U.S.

NORTHWESTERN SALAMANDER
Ambystoma gracile

LOOK FOR: A large, light to dark brown (light brown below) salamander with a big head, prominent glands behind its ears, and a tail with a rough upper surface. SIZE: 5½–8". HABITAT: Moist woodlands, forests, and grasslands. RANGE: Southeastern Alaska to northern California. CAUTION: Skin secretions may be irritating.

SPOTTED SALAMANDER
Ambystoma maculatum

The first warm, rainy night of spring is the time to put on your rubber boots and go out hunting for Spotted Salamanders. These big, yellow-spotted creatures have spent most of the year below ground, waiting for this night to leave their burrows and travel to breeding ponds.

LOOK FOR: A large, blackish salamander with bright yellow to orange spots decorating its upperparts from head to tail; gray below.

EASTERN TIGER SALAMANDER
Ambystoma tigrinum

LOOK FOR: A very large, big-headed salamander with highly variable color patterns; often dark with bold whitish to yellow markings. **SIZE:** 6–12".
HABITAT: Extremely varied, from forests to grasslands. **RANGE:** Widespread in interior U.S.

RINGED SALAMANDER
Ambystoma annulatum

LOOK FOR: A large, blackish salamander with yellow to creamy bands around its body; gray below with light spots. **SIZE:** 5½–8".
HABITAT: Moist woodlands and clearings.
RANGE: Missouri to Arkansas and Oklahoma.

SIZE: 6–8".

HABITAT: Near bodies of water in deciduous forests (with trees that lose their leaves in the fall).

RANGE: Eastern U.S. and southeastern Canada.

MARBLED SALAMANDER
Ambystoma opacum

I n early fall, long after other
mole salamanders have
disappeared from the scene,
Marbled Salamanders mate and
lay their eggs. The eggs are laid in
low areas that have dried out
during the summer. The female

Marbled guards the eggs through
the fall or winter, when rains flood
the eggs and allow them to hatch.

LOOK FOR: A stocky, blackish
salamander with bold white to
silvery crossbands above; male
pattern is brighter; black below.

JEFFERSON SALAMANDER
Ambystoma jeffersonianum

LOOK FOR: A big but slender, long-toed salamander; mostly grayish to dark brown, with tiny bluish flecks on its sides. Tail is flattened on sides. **SIZE:** 4½–8". **HABITAT:** Deciduous woodlands. **RANGE:** Western New England and south to Indiana and Virginia.

BLUE-SPOTTED SALAMANDER
Ambystoma laterale

LOOK FOR: A large, grayish-black to black salamander with many bluish-white to blue flecks on its back and spots on its sides and tail; paler below. **SIZE:** 3–5". **HABITAT:** Deciduous woodlands. **RANGE:** Great Lakes region east to Atlantic Canada.

SIZE: 3½–5".

HABITAT: Moist woodlands near bodies of water.

RANGE: Eastern U.S., south of Great Lakes and most of New England.

111

MOLE SALAMANDER
Ambystoma talpoideum

This species has a confusing name—it is not only a member of the mole salamander family, it is *the* Mole Salamander. Mole Salamanders, like the moles they are named for, are chunky and dark and are very good burrowers. Look for them from December to February.

LOOK FOR: A large, gray to dark

brown salamander with an
unusually large head and legs;
flecked with light blue; bluish-
gray below.

SIZE: 3–4¾".

HABITAT: Deciduous and pine
woodlands and swamps.

RANGE: Eastern Oklahoma and
Texas, east to South Carolina.

SMALLMOUTH SALAMANDER
Ambystoma texanum

LOOK FOR: A large blackish salamander,
usually with a pattern that resembles
lichen (a spongy plant that grows on trees
and plants), and gray blotches above;
black below with tiny light flecks. Both its
head and mouth are extremely small. **SIZE:**
4½–6". **HABITAT:** Moist woodlands; moist
grasslands. **RANGE:** Kansas east to Ohio and
south to Gulf states.

FLATWOODS SALAMANDER
Ambystoma cingulatum

LOOK FOR: A relatively small and slender
mole salamander. Body black with
numerous fine gray bars. **SIZE:** 3½-5".
HABITAT: Pine flatwoods and edges of cypress
swamps. **RANGE:** Southern South Carolina to
southern Alabama.

NORTHERN DUSKY SALAMANDER
Desmognathus fuscus

The dusky salamanders can be identified by the light line that runs from their eyes to the corners of their mouths. This species is the most common dusky salamander. Turning over flat rocks along streams may likely produce several duskies, which can be abundant in places.

LOOK FOR: A brown to gray salamander, with or without a dark-edged back stripe; a light line from its eye to the back of its jaw; the tail is keeled (a raised

SOUTHERN DUSKY SALAMANDER
Desmognathus auriculatus

LOOK FOR: A dark brown to blackish salamander with 2 rows of white to orange spots on each side of its body; dark below with whitish speckles. **SIZE:** 3–6". **HABITAT:** Edges of lakes and streams in lowlands. **RANGE:** Southeastern U.S.

SEAL SALAMANDER
Desmognathus monticola

LOOK FOR: An orange-yellow to light brown salamander with wavy dark markings on back; below, light gray to light brown and usually unmarked. **SIZE:** 4–6". **HABITAT:** Edges of springs and streams. **RANGE:** Pennsylvania to Alabama in Appalachian Mountains.

edge along the tail's upper side).

SIZE: 3–5½".

HABITAT: Springs and streams in woodlands.

RANGE: New Brunswick and Maine south to Louisiana.

PYGMY SALAMANDER
Desmognathus wrighti

Under rotting logs and the mossy bark that covers them dwell the small and handsome Pygmy Salamanders. On very humid nights, they crawl about in the open and sometimes even climb 5 or 6 feet up trees.

LOOK FOR: A tiny salamander with a reddish, herringbone-patterned back stripe and a light line from its eye to its jaw.

SIZE: 1½–2".

HABITAT: Spruce, fir, and deciduous forests.

RANGE: Southwestern Virginia, western North Carolina, and eastern Tennessee.

BLACKBELLY SALAMANDER
Desmognathus quadramaculatus

LOOK FOR: A large, stout, very dark salamander with greenish-gray splotches on its back, light spots on its sides, and a light line from its eye to its jaw; black below. **SIZE:** 4–8". **HABITAT:** Mountain streams, springs, and waterfalls. **RANGE:** West Virginia to Georgia.

ALLEGHENY DUSKY SALAMANDER
Desmognathus ochrophaeus

LOOK FOR: A highly variable species: Color ranges from uniformly dark to striped down the back with yellow, red, or gray. Long, rounded tail is a good identifying mark. **SIZE:** 3–4½". **HABITAT:** Springs and streams at lower elevations; spruce-fir forests in highlands. **RANGE:** New York to Alabama.

117

LONGTAIL SALAMANDER
Eurycea longicauda

The Appalachian Mountains are among the very best places in the world to look for salamanders. There are lots of species and a great many individuals, including the Longtail. As an adult, the Longtail Salamander has a tail about two-thirds its total body length. It is a colorful creature contrasting brightly with the forest floor.

LOOK FOR: A long-tailed, slender salamander with variable markings: a yellow to orange back, orange to blackish sides, and dark spots and bars.

SIZE: 4–7".

HABITAT: Rocky streams, caves, and mines; swamps and low hammocks (raised areas in wetlands) in Florida.

RANGE: Eastern U.S., south from central New York.

NORTHERN TWO-LINED SALAMANDER
Eurycea bislineata

LOOK FOR: A common, orangish salamander with a black-bordered yellow stripe down its back. SIZE: 2½–5". HABITAT: Springs and streams in deciduous woodlands. RANGE: Eastern U.S. and southeastern Canada.

CAVE SALAMANDER
Eurycea lucifuga

LOOK FOR: A slender, long-tailed, orange-colored salamander with abundant dark spots on its upper sides; bigger-headed than similar Longtail Salamander; light and unmarked below. SIZE: 5–7". HABITAT: Limestone caves; also springs. RANGE: East-central U.S.

SPRING SALAMANDER
Gyrinophilus porphyriticus

The line from its eye to its snout separates this big, reddish salamander from its look-alikes. Spring Salamanders can be seen in the spring, but they actually get their name from one of their favorite hangouts—clear mountain springs. They eat a lot of other salamanders.

LOOK FOR: A large, brownish-orange salamander with a unique, dark-edged light line running from its eye to its snout.

SIZE: 4–8".

HABITAT: Cool, clear streams, springs, and caves in highlands.

RANGE: Southern Canada and eastern U.S.

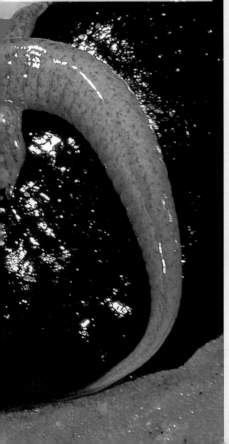

RED SALAMANDER
Pseudotriton ruber

LOOK FOR: A stout, red-orange salamander with numerous black spots and short legs and tail; its eyes are yellow. **SIZE:** 3½–7".
HABITAT: Cold, clear brooks, streams, and nearby areas. **RANGE:** Mid-Atlantic and southeastern U.S.

EASTERN MUD SALAMANDER
Pseudotriton montanus

LOOK FOR: A stout, yellow-orange to brownish-red salamander that resembles the Red Salamander but has dark eyes. **SIZE:** 3–7". **HABITAT:** Muddy streams and swamps. **RANGE:** Southeastern U.S.

GROTTO SALAMANDER
Typhlotriton spelaeus

Most cave-dwelling salamanders that inhabit pools and streams in caves in the southern part of the U.S. are pinkish or beige-colored. This salamander actually starts life in brooks and streams under the sun, but when it transforms to an adult it moves into a cave, loses its larval fins and color, and becomes a blind cave dweller.

LOOK FOR: A pinkish salamander with dark eyes. The larva is brownish with gills and a finned tail.

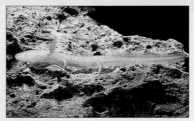

GEORGIA BLIND SALAMANDER
Haideotriton wallacei

LOOK FOR: A pinkish-white aquatic salamander with long red gills and no visible eyes in adults (young have tiny black eyes). **SIZE:** 2–3". **HABITAT:** Limestone cave waters and wells. **RANGE:** Separate populations in southwestern Georgia and nearby Florida.

TENNESSEE CAVE SALAMANDER
Gyrinophilus palleucus

LOOK FOR: A large, pinkish to brownish aquatic salamander with bright red gills, tiny eyes, and a finned tail. **SIZE:** 4–8". **HABITAT:** Limestone cave waters. **RANGE:** Southeastern Tennessee and nearby Alabama and Georgia.

SIZE: 3–5".

HABITAT: Limestone caves as adult; springs and streams as larva.

RANGE: Ozark Mountains of Missouri, Arkansas, and nearby Oklahoma and Kansas.

MOUNT LYELL SALAMANDER
Hydromantes platycephalus

The web-toed salamanders are
found only in California,
where their broad feet help them
climb over rock slabs and cliffs.
Both Mount Lyell and Limestone
Salamanders use their muscular,

LIMESTONE SALAMANDER
Hydromantes brunus

LOOK FOR: A plain brown, web-footed salamander with a flattened body and head and a short tail. **SIZE:** 2½–4¼". **HABITAT:** Mossy limestone cliffs and boulders. **RANGE:** Only in Mariposa County, California.

blunt tails as props and brakes to help them in their rock-climbing.

LOOK FOR: A flattened, web-footed salamander with a short tail; body is color and pattern of granite.

SIZE: 2½–4½".

HABITAT: North-facing, granite mountain slopes.

RANGE: Sierra Nevada mountains in California.

CALIFORNIA SLENDER SALAMANDER
Batrachoseps attenuatus

The rotting logs and ground litter in the great Redwood forests hide some wonderful animals. The California Slender Salamander is one of these creatures. It does not really like to be disturbed in its daytime hiding spot and will flip about crazily when it is uncovered.

LOOK FOR: A very slender, long-tailed salamander with short, skinny legs; the body is dark and the back has a red to yellowish stripe; each foot has 4 toes.

SIZE: 3–5".

HABITAT: Mountain and foothill woodlands; also grasslands.

RANGE: California and southwestern Oregon.

RELICTUAL SLENDER SALAMANDER
Batrachoseps relictus

LOOK FOR: A slender, dark-bodied salamander with a variably colored back stripe; each foot has 4 toes. **SIZE:** 2½–4⅓". **HABITAT:** Edges of springs and small streams in chaparral and pine and oak woods. **RANGE:** Central California.

OREGON SLENDER SALAMANDER
Batrachoseps wrightorum

LOOK FOR: A slender, dark-bodied salamander with a yellowish to red-brown back stripe and 4 toes on each foot; black below with large white spots. **SIZE:** 3¼–4¼". **HABITAT:** Near springs in moist woodlands. **RANGE:** Central Oregon.

127

Up in the mountains, Dunn's Salamanders are inactive in the cold, winter months. In the lowlands, however, they can be found year-round and are especially active in April. The Dunn's is more at home in water than many other woodland salamanders.

Look for: A woodland salamander with a greenish (usually) to light brown back stripe that does not reach its tail tip; dark gray below with yellowish flecks.

Size: 4–5½".

Habitat: Moss-covered logs and rocks.

Range: Western Oregon and nearby Washington and California.

WESTERN REDBACK SALAMANDER
Plethodon vehiculum

Look for: A common woodland salamander with a variably colored (red, orange, yellow, tan, or dusky) back stripe that runs to the end of its tail; gray below with light flecks. **Size:** 2½–4¼". **Habitat:** Moist woodlands. **Range:** Southern British Columbia to western Oregon.

VAN DYKE'S SALAMANDER
Plethodon vandykei

Look for: A variably colored salamander with distinct glands at the back of its head; the back stripe is tan, reddish, or yellow. **Size:** 3¾–4½". **Habitat:** Moist open areas and forests near streams and lakes. **Range:** Western Washington and northern Idaho and Montana.

LARCH MOUNTAIN SALAMANDER
Plethodon larselli

This small salamander shares its habitat with poisonous millipedes, which coil up when they are uncovered under forest debris. Larch Mountain Salamanders also coil up and some herpetologists think they are mimicking the toxic millipedes and hoping to fool predators.

LOOK FOR: The smallest western woodland salamander; the back stripe is tan, reddish, or yellowish; body is pink, red, or red-orange below.

DEL NORTE SALAMANDER
Plethodon elongatus

LOOK FOR: A dark, long-bodied salamander with tiny white or yellow spots on its sides and belly; may or may not have a red to orange-brown back stripe. **SIZE:** 4½–6". **HABITAT:** Rocky slopes in coniferous forests. **RANGE:** Southwestern Oregon to northwestern California.

JEMEZ MOUNTAINS SALAMANDER
Plethodon neomexicanus

LOOK FOR: A long-bodied, dark salamander with small, gold spots on its back; dark below. **SIZE:** 2½–5". **HABITAT:** Moist evergreen forests, mostly under rotting logs and rocks. **RANGE:** Jemez Mountains, New Mexico.

SIZE: 3–4".

HABITAT: Low-elevation rocky slopes, mostly in Douglas Fir forests.

RANGE: Columbia River Gorge in Washington and Oregon.

131

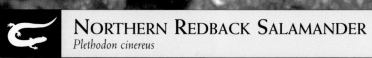
This is the most abundant animal with bones in the Northeast woodlands. Redbacks come in three color phases: red-striped "redback," dark-striped "leadback," and a rare, red-bodied phase. Mites, which are also abundant, are one of their most important foods.

LOOK FOR: A very common, slender, dark salamander with or without a yellowish to reddish back stripe; dark below with light spots.

SIZE: 2½–4¼".

HABITAT: Under stones, logs, and moist leaf litter in woods.

RANGE: Southeastern Canada and south to North Carolina.

RAVINE SALAMANDER
Plethodon richmondi

LOOK FOR: A slender, dark brown to blackish salamander with tiny silver and gold flakes on its upper sides; dark below. **SIZE:** 3–5".
HABITAT: Wooded highland slopes. **RANGE:** Indiana and Ohio, south to North Carolina.

ZIGZAG SALAMANDER
Plethodon dorsalis

LOOK FOR: A slender salamander with a yellowish to red back stripe that is wavy, at least at the front half; black, white, and orange below. **SIZE:** 2½–4". **HABITAT:** Moist, rocky areas in deciduous woodlands. **RANGE:** Indiana and Ohio, south to Louisiana and Mississippi.

NORTHERN SLIMY SALAMANDER
Plethodon glutinosus

Think twice before you reach out to pick up a Northern Slimy Salamander. The "slime" that gives them their common name is actually more like glue than slime. You will be lucky to get it off your hands after a few days of hand-washing.

LOOK FOR: A large, shiny black salamander with white to creamy spots (largest on its sides) scattered

WEHRLE'S SALAMANDER
Plethodon wehrlei

LOOK FOR: A brown to dark gray salamander with white, yellow, or light blue spots and small patches along the sides of its body; dark below, except for whitish throat. **SIZE:** 4–6". **HABITAT:** Rock crevices and cave mouths in Appalachian woodlands. **RANGE:** New York and south to North Carolina.

JORDAN'S SALAMANDER
Plethodon jordani

LOOK FOR: A common, dark gray to blackish salamander; may be plain or have bright red cheeks or red thighs in parts of range. **SIZE:** 3–7". **HABITAT:** Moist slopes of Appalachian woodlands. **RANGE:** Southern Virginia to northern Georgia.

over its upperparts; dark below. Its skin is very sticky.

SIZE: 4½–8".

HABITAT: Moist woodland hillsides and other woodland sites.

RANGE: Mid-Atlantic and southeastern U.S.

CAUTION: Skin secretions very sticky.

YONAHLOSSEE SALAMANDER
Plethodon yonahlossee

The Yonahlossee Salamander is both extremely handsome and extremely quick. As soon as you see it you will recognize it, but as soon as it sees you it will try to get down into its burrow as fast as it can. It got its interesting name from the first place it was discovered, on Yonahlossee Road on Grandfather Mountain in North Carolina.

LOOK FOR: A striking salamander with 3 main colors: a red back, light gray sides, and a dark head, tail, and underside.

RICH MOUNTAIN SALAMANDER
Plethodon ouachitae

LOOK FOR: A variably colored salamander; often blackish with some chestnut color above and whitish spots on its sides; dark below with a whitish throat. **SIZE:** 4–6".
HABITAT: Cool, moist slopes in deciduous woodlands. **RANGE:** Ouachita Mountains, Arkansas and Oklahoma.

SIZE: 4½–7".

HABITAT: Mountain hillsides and ravines with deciduous woods.

RANGE: Southern Blue Ridge Mountains, Virginia to North Carolina.

ARBOREAL SALAMANDER
Aneides lugubris

Arboreal means "of the trees," and it is the perfect name for this salamander, which gets beneath the loose bark of trees and climbs all over the place. Arboreal Salamanders often climb trees to heights of 30 or more feet, and one was once found 60 feet up.

CLOUDED SALAMANDER
Aneides ferreus

LOOK FOR: A tree-climbing salamander with a brown back "clouded" with greenish, bronzy, or silver markings; gray to brown with white spots below. **SIZE:** 3–5". **HABITAT:** Redwood and other coniferous forests. **RANGE:** Coastal Oregon and northern California.

BLACK SALAMANDER
Aneides flavipunctatus

LOOK FOR: A black salamander with or without small white spots above; grayish-black below. **SIZE:** 3½–6". **HABITAT:** Varied, from grasslands to evergreen woodlands. **RANGE:** Northwestern California and nearby Oregon.

LOOK FOR: A tree-climbing, brown-backed salamander; creamy white below.

SIZE: 4–7".

HABITAT: Various woodlands, from oak to pine.

RANGE: Coast Ranges and Sierra Nevada foothills in California.

GREEN SALAMANDER
Aneides aeneus

Like its western cousins, the Green Salamander—the only eastern climbing salamander—has a flat head and body, the perfect body design for sneaking into tight cracks and crevices on cliffs. Even when they are not hiding, Green Salamanders can be hard to see; their bodies are patterned like lichen (a spongelike plant that grows on trees and rocks), which camouflages them on the rocky habitats where they roam.

SACRAMENTO MOUNTAIN SALAMANDER
Aneides hardii

LOOK FOR: The only North American salamander found in tundra. Brown to blackish above with light brown to gray-green markings. Active only in midsummer, when temperature permits.
SIZE: 3–4½". **HABITAT:** Evergreen forests and tundra regions at high elevations.
RANGE: Sacramento, White, and Capitan mountains, New Mexico.

LOOK FOR: A gray to dark brown salamander with a flattened head and body and green to yellow-green splotches on its uppersides; pale yellowish below.

SIZE: 3–5".

HABITAT: Moist rock faces with narrow cracks in hardwood forests.

RANGE: Southwestern Pennsylvania and south to Alabama and South Carolina.

ENSATINA
Ensatina eschscholtzii

The Ensatina is an easy salamander to find, but a little hard to describe, since it seems to look so different from place to place. One common feature of all Ensatinas is the narrow base of the tail. If its tail snaps off when an Ensatina is trying to escape a predator, it will grow back, although it takes about two years to reach its full size again.

LOOK FOR: A striking salamander with enormous variety of colors. Reddish to brown to black above, often

yellow to orange at base of legs. Tail distinctly narrow at base.

Size: 3–5½".

Habitat: Under rotting logs and rocks in various forests.

Range: Southern British Columbia and south to California.

LARGE-BLOTCHED RACE

FOUR-TOED SALAMANDER
Hemidactylium scutatum

In the boggy areas where meat-eating pitcher plants and sundews try to make a living, Four-toed Salamanders crawl about in the soggy moss. Give yourself a pat on the back when you find a Four-toed—it means you've been trying hard!

LOOK FOR: A small salamander with 4 toes on its hind feet, a reddish back, gray sides, and narrowing at the base of its tail; whitish below

with black spots.

SIZE: 2–4".

HABITAT: Mossy areas in bogs and other wetlands.

RANGE: Eastern U.S.

DWARF SALAMANDER
Eurycea quadridigitata

LOOK FOR: A small, brown-backed salamander with 4 toes on its hind feet; a blackish stripe runs down the back from behind each eye. **SIZE:** 2–3½". **HABITAT:** Pond edges in lowland pine and deciduous woods. **RANGE:** Southeastern U.S.

MANY-LINED SALAMANDER
Stereochilus marginatus

LOOK FOR: A yellow-brown salamander with numerous fine light and dark streaks along its sides; back normally plain; belly yellowish with small dark spots. **SIZE:** 2½–4½". **HABITAT:** Cypress swamps, ponds. **RANGE:** Virginia to Georgia.

AQUATIC ADULT

While many salamanders live their young lives in water and their adult lives on land, Eastern Newts start out in water, then spend two to seven years on land as brightly colored Red Efts, before returning to water to mature into aquatic adults. The water-bound adults remain active year-round and can sometimes even be seen swimming under ice. They are also called Red-spotted Newts.

LOOK FOR: Two distinct stages: Adults are olive above, yellowish below, with black-outlined red spots above and small black spots all over; efts are reddish-orange all

STRIPED NEWT
Notophthalmus perstriatus

LOOK FOR: Two distinct stages: Adults are olive to dark brown above, yellow with black spots below; efts are reddish orange. Both adult and eft have a red stripe along each side of the body. **SIZE:** 2–3½". **HABITAT:** Ponds, ditches, and nearby woodlands. **RANGE:** Southern Georgia to central Florida.

BLACK-SPOTTED NEWT
Notophthalmus meridionalis

LOOK FOR: An aquatic newt covered with small black spots. Dark olive above, yellow to orange below, with broken yellow stripe down center of back. No eft stage. **SIZE:** 3–4". **HABITAT:** Ponds, streams, and ditches. **RANGE:** Southern Texas.

over, with black-outlined red spots on their backs.

SIZE: 2½–5".

HABITAT: Adults in ponds; efts on moist leaves and under cover in moist woods.

RANGE: Southeastern Canada and eastern U.S.

ROUGHSKIN NEWT
Taricha granulosa

Roughskin Newts are more commonly seen than any other salamander in the Northwest. If they are disturbed, they arch their backs and raise their heads and tails, exposing the bright colors of their undersides.

More than most salamanders, Roughskin Newts wander about in bright daylight.

LOOK FOR: A large, warty-skinned newt; brown to black above, yellow to orange below. Breeding males have smooth skin.

CALIFORNIA NEWT
Taricha torosa

LOOK FOR: A large newt, very similar to Roughskin Newt but with light lower eyelids and bigger eyes. **SIZE:** 5–7½". **HABITAT:** Ponds, streams, and nearby woodlands. **RANGE:** California.

REDBELLY NEWT
Taricha rivularis

LOOK FOR: A large, blackish newt with a fire-red belly and large eyes. **SIZE:** 5½–7½". **HABITAT:** Fast, cool streams in Redwood forests. **RANGE:** Northern coastal California.

SIZE: 5–8".

HABITAT: Ponds and streams and nearby moist grasslands and woodlands.

RANGE: Southeastern Alaska to central California.

Bullfrog page 96

How to use the reference section

The **Glossary,** which begins below, contains terms used by herpetologists and naturalists. If you run across a word in this book that you do not understand, check the glossary for a definition. Also in this section is a listing of **Resources,** including books, CDs, organizations, and Web sites devoted to North American amphibians, as well as a table for learning how to convert measurements to metrics. Finally, there is an **Index** of all the species covered in the field guide section of this book.

GLOSSARY

Aquatic
Found in water.

Arid
Extremely dry.

Bayou
A marshy and slow-moving body of water.

Bleat
A cry like the sound a sheep makes.

Bog
A wetland with spongelike mosses and carnivorous plants.

Breed
To produce offspring.

Brushland
A dry habitat with low-growing plants and shrubs.

Burrow
To dig a hole or tunnel in the ground for shelter.

Camouflage
Colors or patterns that help animals blend in with their environments.

Chaparral
A dry habitat of dense evergreen shrubs and small trees. Most common on hillsides of California.

Climate
The average weather in a certain place or during a certain season.

Coastal plain
A flat region that runs along a coastline.

Conifer
A tree that bears cones, such as a pine or spruce.

Cypress
A type of conifer. Cypress swamps and bays are wetlands with cypress trees.

Deciduous
Describes trees that lose all their leaves in fall or winter.

Eft
The phase a newt goes through before adulthood when it lives on land.

Endangered
In danger of becoming extinct.

Evergreen
Describes trees that keep their leaves year-round.

Evolve
To change from generation to generation. Living things evolve through time; this is how new species develop.

Extinct
Describes a plant or animal species that has died out completely.

Floodplain
A flat area of land that is sometimes covered by floodwaters.

Foothills
Hills at the bottom of bigger hills or mountains.

Genus (plural: genera)
A group of closely related species.

Gills
Organs located on the sides of the neck that larval and some adult amphibians use to breathe underwater.

Grassland
An area of prairie or meadow grass, usually on flat or rolling plains that are dry most of the year.

Habitat
The environment in which an animal lives.

Herpetologist
A scientist who studies amphibians and reptiles.

Hibernation
A long, deep sleep, usually over the winter, when an animal's heartbeat and breathing slow down and its body temperature drops.

Introduced
Describes a species that has been brought from one area to an area that it had not lived in before.

Keel
A narrow, raised ridge. Some salamanders have a keel along the upper edge of the tail.

Larva (plural: larvae)
A young animal, such as a tadpole, that has hatched from its egg but must go through other growth stages before it becomes an adult.

Marsh
A shallow, treeless wetland that develops around slow-moving bodies of water.

Metamorphosis
The process by which larvae change into adults, as when a tadpole turns into a frog.

Native
Describes a plant or animal species that originated in a particular region.

Nocturnal
Active at night.

Population
A group of animals of a species living in a particular area. Animals are sometimes found living in small, isolated populations.

Predator
An animal that hunts and kills other animals for food.

Prey
An animal caught by predators for food.

Pupil
The opening in the eye that controls the intake of light by opening and closing.

Range
The geographic area where a species normally lives.

Sageland
A western habitat mostly made up of small, gray-green shrubs called sage.

Scrubland
A desert habitat with thick, dense areas of small trees and shrubs.

Species
Animals that look alike and can mate and produce young.

Subspecies
Animals of the same species that can be separated into even smaller groups by their appearance or by where they live.

Trill
A sound repeated over and over through vibration.

Tundra
A treeless plain of very cold regions, such as arctic Canada; also a treeless area on mountain tops.

Vegetation
Plant life.

Vertebrate
An animal with a backbone.

Vocal sac
The pouch on the throat of male frogs and toads that expands when they make their calls.

Wash
A very shallow body of water, usually in a dry area.

RESOURCES

Western Spadefoot (page 61) digging into a burrow

FOR FURTHER READING

Amazing Frogs and Toads
(Eyewitness Juniors)
Barry Clarke
Alfred A. Knopf, 1990

Amphibian
(Eyewitness Books)
Barry Clarke
Alfred A. Knopf, 1993

A Field Guide to Reptiles and Amphibians: Eastern and Central North America
(Peterson Field Guides)
Roger Conant and Joseph Collins
Houghton Mifflin, 1998

A Field Guide to Western Reptiles and Amphibians
(Peterson Field Guides)
Robert C. Stebbins
Houghton Mifflin, 1985

Frogs
(First Discovery Book)
Daniel Moignot
Gallimard Jeunesse
Scholastic Inc., 1997

Frogs, Frogs Everywhere
(Creatures All Around Us)
D. M. Souza
Carolrhoda Books, 1994

Frogs, Toads, Lizards, and Salamanders
Nancy W. Parker and Joan R. Wright
Mulberry Books, 1996

A Guide to Amphibians and Reptiles
(Stokes Nature Guides)
Thomas F. Tyning, Donald W. Stokes, and Lillian Q. Stokes
Little, Brown & Co., 1990

Let's Hear It for Herps
(Ranger Rick's Naturescope Guides)
National Wildlife Federation
McGraw-Hill, 1997

National Audubon Society Field Guide to North American Reptiles and Amphibians
John L. Behler and F. Wayne King
Alfred A. Knopf, 1979

National Audubon Society Pocket Guide to Familiar Reptiles and Amphibians
John L. Behler
Alfred A. Knopf, 1988

Red-spotted Newt
Doris Gove and Beverly Duncan
Atheneum, 1994

Salamanders
Emery Bernhard and Durga Bernhard
Holiday House, 1995

Salamanders
(Nature Watch Book)
Cherie Winner
First Avenue Editions, 1993

Shy Salamanders
D. M. Souza
Carolrhoda Books, 1994

What is an Amphibian?
Robert Snedden
Little, Brown & Co., 1994

TAPES AND DISKS

Amphibian
(Eyewitness Videos)
Dorling Kindersley

The Calls of Frogs and Toads
(Audio CD)
Lang Elliott
NatureSound Studio
Northwood Press, 1994

Frog Concertos
(Audio CD)
Lang Elliott and Ted Mack
NatureSound Studio

The Frog Pond
(Audio cassette)
Droll Yankees

ORGANIZATIONS

Defenders of Wildlife
1101 14th Street NW, #1400
Washington, DC 20005
Tel: 202-682-9400
http://www.defenders.org

EarthWatch International
680 Mount Auburn Street
P.O. Box 403
Watertown, MA 02272
Tel: 800-776-0188
http://www.earthwatch.org

National Audubon Society
700 Broadway
New York, NY 10003-9562
Tel: 212-979-3000
http://www.audubon.org/

National Wildlife Federation
8925 Leesburg Pike
Vienna, VA 22184
Tel: 703-970-4100
http://www.nwf.org

The Nature Conservancy
International Headquarters
1815 North Lynn Street
Arlington, VA 22209
Tel: 703-841-5300
http://www.tnc.org

Sierra Club
85 2nd Street, 2nd Floor
San Francisco, CA
94105-3441
Tel: 415-977-5500
http://www.sierraclub.org

Wildlife Conservation Society
Bronx Zoo
Bronx, New York 10460
Tel: 718-220-5152
http://www.wcs.org

WEB SITES

The Amphibian Reference:
http://newts.org/~newto

Audubon's "Educate Yourself" Web site:
http://www.audubon.org/educate

The Basking Spot:
http://www.baskingspot.com

The Electronic Zoo:
http://netvet.wustl.edu/e-zoo.htm

The Froggy Page:
http://frog.simplenet.com/froggy

Herp Link:
http://www.home.ptd.net/~herplink/index.html

National Wildlife Federation's Kid's Page:
http://www.nwf.org/kids

Terra:
http://www.olcommerce.com/terra/reptile.html

Make it metric

Here is a chart you can use to change measurements of size, distance, weight, and temperature to their metric equivalents.

	multiply by
inches to millimeters	25
inches to centimeters	2.5
feet to meters	0.3
yards to meters	0.9
miles to kilometers	1.6
square miles to square kilometers	2.6
ounces to grams	28.3
pounds to kilograms	.45
Fahrenheit to Centigrade	subtract 32 and multiply by .55

INDEX

Page numbers in **bold type** point to an object's page in the field guide.

An amphibian search

INDEX

Southern Toad page 71

Van Dyke's Salamanders, page 129

PHOTO CREDITS

Front cover: C. Allan Morgan
Half-title (Eastern Spadefoot):
Suzanne L. Collins & Joseph T.
Collins/Photo Researchers*
Title page (Slimy Salamander):
R. W. Van Devender
Table of Contents (Tree Frog):
Anthony Mercieca/Photo
Researchers
6: E. R. Degginger/Color-Pic, Inc.
8a: Marvalee and David Wake
8b: Karl H. Switak
10a: William P. Leonard
10b: Jack Dermid
11a: Breck P. Kent
11b: R. D. Bartlett
11c: Suzanne L. Collins/CNAAR
11d: David M. Dennis
12a: Phil A. Dotson/Photo
Researchers
12b (Little Grass Frog): Index
Stock Photography
12c (Oxeye Daisy): Patrick W.
Grace/Photo Researchers
12d: C. Allan Morgan
13a: Breck P. Kent
13b: Brian Kenney
14: David Northcott
15a: R. D. Bartlett
15b: Breck P. Kent
15c: E. R. Degginger/Color-Pic,
Inc.
16–17 (Northern Leopard Frog):
Suzanne L. Collins & Joseph T.
Collins/CNAAR
16a: R. D. Bartlett
16b: Allen Blake Sheldon
16c: William P. Leonard
17a: David Northcott
17b: James H. Robinson
17c: Joseph T. Collins/Photo
Researchers
17d: Breck P. Kent
18–19: R. D. Bartlett
18a: Jack Dermid
18b: Breck P. Kent
18c: E. R. Degginger/Photo
Researchers
19a: Allen Blake Sheldon
19b: Phil A. Dotson/Photo
Researchers
19c: R. D. Bartlett
20–21: Allen Blake Sheldon
20a: William P. Leonard
20b: Joe McDonald

21a: Breck P. Kent
21b: Leonard Lee Rue III/Photo
Researchers
22–23: Ted Levin
22a: Karl H. Switak
22b: William P. Leonard
23: Dan Suzio
24–25: Breck P. Kent
24a: Dan Suzio
24b: Dan Suzio
24c: Dan Suzio
25a: Dan Suzio
25b: Dan Suzio
25c: Dan Suzio
26–27: Ted Levin
26a: John Mitchell/Photo
Researchers
27a: Karl H. Switak
27b: Breck P. Kent
27c: Tom Tyning
28–29: John Serrao/Photo
Researchers
28a: Dennis Sheridan
29a: R. D. Bartlett
30–31: A. Cosmos Blank/Photo
Researchers
30a: R. D. Bartlett
31a: Kenneth H. Thomas/Photo
Researchers
31b: Joe McDonald
32–33: Stephen Dalton/Photo
Researchers
32a: Allen Blake Sheldon
32b: Breck P. Kent
33a: R. D. Bartlett
33b: Phil A. Dotson/Photo
Researchers
34a: E. R. Degginger/Color-Pic,
Inc.
34b: Dennis Sheridan
35a: Bill Beatty
35b: R. D. Bartlett
35c: Byron Jorjorian
35d: C. Allan Morgan.
36a: Joe McDonald
36b (top background):
Allen Blake Sheldon
36c: R. D. Bartlett
36d (bottom background):
John Elk III
37a: William P. Leonard
37b (top background):
William P. Leonard
37c: Charles K. Webb
37d (bottom background):
George Ranalli/Photo
Researchers
38a: Ernie Cooper/Ursus

Photography
38b (top background):
David M. Dennis
38c: Allen Blake Sheldon
38d (bottom background):
John Elk III
39a: Karl H. Switak
39b (top background): Gregory
Ochocki/Photo Researchers
39c: Joe McDonald
39d (bottom background):
Paul Rezendes
40: Byron Jorjorian
41: William P. Leonard
42–43: William P. Leonard
42a: William P. Leonard
42b: William P. Leonard
43a: William P. Leonard
44–45: Jack Dermid
44a: Breck P. Kent
45a: Ted Levin
46–47: Karl H. Switak
46–47 (background):
Karl H. Switak
46a: William P. Leonard
47a: R. D. Bartlett
47b: R. D. Bartlett
47c: Dan Suzio
48a: Dan Suzio
48b: Joe McDonald
50: Allen Blake Sheldon
51a: Allen Blake Sheldon
51b: Suzanne L. Collins & Joseph
T. Collins/Photo Researchers
52: Suzanne L. Collins & Joseph T.
Collins/Photo Researchers
53a: Suzanne L. Collins & Joseph T.
Collins/Photo Researchers
53b: Karl H. Switak/Photo
Researchers
54: Joseph T. Collins/Photo
Researchers
55a: R. D. Bartlett
55b: R. D. Bartlett
56–57: William P. Leonard
56a (inset): William P. Leonard
58–59: Joe McDonald
59a: E. R. Degginger/Color-Pic,
Inc.
60: Phil Degginger/Color-Pic, Inc.
61a: Joseph T. Collins/Photo
Researchers
61b: C. Allan Morgan
62: William P. Leonard
62a (inset): R. D. Bartlett
63a: Allen Blake Sheldon
63b: William P. Leonard
64: William P. Leonard

65a: Breck P. Kent
65b: David Northcott
66: R. D. Bartlett
67a: David Northcott
67b: C. Allan Morgan
68: E. R. Degginger/Color-Pic, Inc.
69a: Mark Warner
69b: Joseph T. Collins/Photo
  Researchers
70: James C. Godwin
71a: Mark Smith
71b: R. D. Bartlett
72: Suzanne L. & Joseph T.
  Collins/Photo Researchers
73a: R. D. Bartlett
73b: David Northcott
74–75: Breck P. Kent
75a: Allen Blake Sheldon
76: Karl H. Switak
77a: Breck P. Kent
77b: Gilbert S. Grant/Photo
  Researchers
78: David Liebman
79a: Joe McDonald
79b: E. R. Degginger/Color-Pic,
  Inc.
80: E. R. Degginger/Color-Pic, Inc.
81a: Brian Kenney
81b: Joe McDonald
82: Brian Kenney
83a: Karl H. Switak
83b: Tom McHugh/Photo
  Researchers
84: Jack Dermid
85a: R. D. Bartlett
85b: Allen Blake Sheldon
86: R. D. Bartlett
87a: Jack Dermid
87b: Jack Dermid
88: Karl H. Switak
89a: R. D. Bartlett
89b: Stephen Ingram
90–91: William P. Leonard
91a: William P. Leonard
92: Stephen G. Maka
93a: Breck P. Kent
93b: William P. Leonard
94: Breck P. Kent
95a: Allen Blake Sheldon
95b: Jack Dermid
96: Michael P. Gadomski/Photo
  Researchers
97a: John Serrao
97b: R. D. Bartlett
98: E. R. Degginger/Color-Pic, Inc.
99a: R. D. Bartlett
99b: R. D. Bartlett
100–101: R.J. Erwin/Photo

Researchers
102: R. D. Bartlett
103a: Jack Dermid
103b: Jack Dermid
104–105: Phil A. Dotson/Photo
  Researchers
105a: E. R. Degginger/Color-Pic,
  Inc.
106: Karl H. Switak
107a: Joseph T. Collins/Photo
  Researchers
107b: William P. Leonard
108: Brian Kenney
109a: R. D. Bartlett
109b: Allen Blake Sheldon
110: Allen Blake Sheldon
111a: Jack Dermid
111b: Allen Blake Sheldon
112: Allen Blake Sheldon
113a: Allen Blake Sheldon
113b: R. D. Bartlett
114: Jack Dermid
115a: E. R. Degginger/Color-Pic,
  Inc.
115b: E. R. Degginger/Color-Pic,
  Inc.
116: R. D. Bartlett
117a: Jack Dermid
117b: Allen Blake Sheldon
118: Jack Dermid
119a: Bill Beatty
119b: Allen Blake Sheldon
120: Jack Dermid
121a: Allen Blake Sheldon
121b: Jack Dermid
122: Joseph T. Collins/Photo
  Researchers
123a: David M. Dennis
123b: John MacGregor/CNAAR
124–125: William P. Leonard
125a: Robert W. Hansen/CNAAR
126: William P. Leonard
127a: Robert W. Hansen/CNAAR
127b: William P. Leonard
128: William P. Leonard
129a: Jim Yuskavitch
129b: David M. Dennis
130: William P. Leonard
131a: R. D. Bartlett
131b: Suzanne L. Collins & Joseph
  T. Collins/CNAAR
132: Allen Blake Sheldon
133a: Dr. G. J. Chafaris/Color-Pic,
  Inc.
133b: Jack Dermid
134: Breck P. Kent
135a: Jack Dermid
135b: Allen Blake Sheldon

136–137: Allen Blake Sheldon
137a: R. D. Bartlett
138: Dennis Sheridan
139a: William P. Leonard
139b: David M. Dennis
140–141: R. D. Bartlett
141a: Larry Miller/Photo
  Researchers
142–143: Karl H. Switak
143a (inset): R. D. Bartlett
144: R. D. Bartlett
145a: Joseph T. Collins/Photo
  Researchers
145b: Joseph T. Collins/Photo
  Researchers
146: Brian Kenney
146a (inset): Jack Dermid
147a: R. D. Bartlett
147b: R. D. Bartlett
148: Vaughan Photography
149a: Breck P. Kent
149b: R. D. Bartlett
150–151 (background):
  Karl H. Switak
150a: Michael Lustbader/Photo
  Researchers
152a: Karl H. Switak
152b: Karl H. Switak
154–155: Suzanne L.
  Collins/CNAAR
156: Breck P. Kent
157: Joe McDonald

*Photo Researchers, Inc.
60 East 56th Street
New York, NY 10022

159

Prepared and produced by
Chanticleer Press, Inc.

Publisher: Andrew Stewart
Founder: Paul Steiner

Chanticleer Staff:
Editor-in-Chief: Amy K. Hughes
Senior Editor: Miriam Harris
Managing Editor: George Scott
Associate Editor: Michelle Bredeson
Assistant Editor: Elizabeth Wright
Editorial Assistants: Amy Oh, Anne O'Connor
Photo Director: Zan Carter
Photo Editors: Ruth Jeyaveeran, Jennifer McClanaghan
Assistant Photo Editor: Meg Kuhta
Rights and Permissions Manager: Alyssa Sachar
Photo Assistants: Leslie Fink, Karin Murphy
Art Director: Drew Stevens
Designers: Kirsten Berger, Brian Boyce, Anthony Liptak,
Vincent Mejia, Bernadette Vibar
Director of Production: Alicia Mills
Production Manager: Philip Pfeifer

Contributors:
Writer: Brian Cassie
Text Consultant: Thomas F. Tyning
Photo Consultant: John L. Behler
Icons: Holly Kowitt

Scholastic Inc. Staff:
Editorial Director: Wendy Barish, Creative Director: David Saylor,
Managing Editor: Manuela Soares, Manufacturing Manager: Karen Fuchs

Original Series Design: Chic Simple Design